W9-AAZ-275

THE MUSIC LIBRARY

The History of American Pop

Stuart A. Kallen

LUCENT BOOKS
A part of Gale, Cengage Learning

GALE
CENGAGE Learning™

Detroit • New York • San Francisco • New Haven, Conn • Waterville, Maine • London

LIBRARY OF CONGRESS CATALOGING-IN-PUBLICATION DATA

Kallen, Stuart A., 1955-
    The history of American pop / by Stuart A. Kallen.
      p. cm. -- (The music library)
    Includes bibliographical references and index.
    ISBN 978-1-4205-0672-3 (hardcover)
   1. Popular music--United States--History and criticism--Juvenile literature. I. Title.
    ML3477.K34 2012
    781.640973--dc23

                                2011029991

Lucent Books
27500 Drake Rd
Farmington Hills MI 48331

ISBN-13: 978-1-4205-0672-3
ISBN-10: 1-4205-0672-2

Printed in the United States of America
2 3 4 5 6 7 15 14 13 12

CONTENTS

FOREWORD

In the nineteenth century, English novelist Charles Kingsley wrote, "Music speaks straight to our hearts and spirits, to the very core and root of our souls. . . . Music soothes us, stirs us up . . . melts us to tears." As Kingsley stated, music is much more than just a pleasant arrangement of sounds. It is the resonance of emotion, a joyful noise, a human endeavor that can soothe the spirit or excite the soul. Musicians can also imitate the expressive palette of the earth, from the violent fury of a hurricane to the gentle flow of a babbling brook.

The word *music* is derived from the fabled Greek muses, the children of Apollo who ruled the realms of inspiration and imagination. Composers have long called upon the muses for help and insight. Music is not merely the result of emotions and pleasurable sensations, however.

Music is a discipline subject to formal study and analysis. It involves the juxtaposition of creative elements such as rhythm, melody, and harmony with intellectual aspects of composition, theory, and instrumentation. Like painters mixing red, blue, and yellow into thousands of colors, musicians blend these various elements to create classical symphonies, jazz improvisations, country ballads, and rock-and-roll tunes.

Throughout centuries of musical history, individual musical elements have been blended and modified in infinite ways. The resulting sounds may convey a whole range of moods, emotions, reactions, and messages. Music, then, is both an expression and reflection of human experience and emotion.

The foundations of modern musical styles were laid down by the first ancient musicians who used wood, rocks, animal skins—and their own bodies—to re-create the sounds of the natural world in which they lived. With their hands, their feet, and their very breath they ignited the passions of listeners and moved them to their feet. The dancing, in turn, had a mesmerizing and hypnotic effect that allowed people to transcend their worldly concerns. Through music they could achieve a level of shared experience that could not be found in other forms of communication. For this reason, music has always been part of religious endeavors, from ancient Egyptian spiritual ceremonies to modern Christian masses. And it has inspired dance movements from kings and queens spinning the minuet to punk rockers slamming together in a mosh pit.

By examining musical genres ranging from Western classical music to rock and roll, readers will find a new understanding of old music and develop an appreciation for new sounds. Books in Lucent's Music Library focus on the music, the musicians, the instruments, and on music's place in cultural history. The songs and artists examined may be easily found in the CD and sheet music collections of local libraries so that readers may study and enjoy the music covered in the books. Informative sidebars, annotated bibliographies, and complete indexes highlight the text in each volume and provide young readers with many opportunities for further discussion and research.

Popular Music

In the twenty-first century, music lovers have instant access to millions of songs in hundreds of musical styles. From ragtime to jazz and blues to rap, nearly every American song genre is available with the click of a computer mouse. Popular digital download stores like iTunes and Rhapsody have more than 10 million songs available, and that number is growing every day. Whether the tunes are rock and roll, hip hop, soul, or rhythm and blues (R&B), many of them are classified as American pop, a broad musical style that has dominated the aural landscape since the late 1800s.

The term *pop* was first used in the 1920s to define American songs that had popular appeal. During this era, songs became popular as a result of two forces, records and radio. Record companies, which had been producing records since the late 1890s, promoted many beloved musical styles to keep the public buying new releases. Some of the best-selling pop genres included ragtime, blues, jazz, Broadway show tunes, patriotic songs, sentimental ballads, and country, or hillbilly music.

Radios were first mass-produced in 1920, and by the 1930s almost every American household owned one. National stations played popular records that were heard from coast to coast. The synergy of radio and records in the

1920s helped the music industry sell more than 100 million records annually in the United States.

Popular tastes changed from year to year and musical styles were constantly created, combined, and reinvented to produce new genres. As a result, modern pop music has grown to include folk, swing, rock, country, R&B, soul, punk, alternative, disco, grunge, and hip hop. Some of the styles, such as hip hop and grunge, started out as rebellious music made by those who lived on the margins of society. Because millions of music lovers could relate to the central messages behind these songs, they became popular and defined as pop music.

Romance and Rebellion

Pop songs often appeal to a listener's feelings and self-identity and trigger pleasant memories. Larry Starr, a professor of music, and Christopher Waterman, a professor of arts and culture, explain the power of pop:

> As we move into adolescence, popular music ... enters into our private lives, providing comfort and continuity during emotional crises and offering the opportunity to fantasize about romance and rebellion. . . . As you grow older, a song or a singer's voice may suddenly transport you back to a specific moment and place in your life, sometimes decades earlier.[1]

The ability to prompt daydreams and nostalgia makes pop music an attractive escape from the harsh realities of daily living. It provides a sound track to peoples' lives that entwines emotion with experience. It is little wonder that eventful periods in American history are defined by the pop music of the time. For example, big band jazz from the 1940s evokes memories of World War II for those who lived through that era, while songs from the 1960s often remind baby boomers of the drug-fueled hippie revolution.

Spanning the Globe

While American pop originated in the United States, the music now spans the globe. People on every continent are familiar with musicians like Hank Williams, Elvis Presley, Bob Dylan, Dolly Parton, Madonna, 50 Cent, Lady Gaga, and Justin Bieber. The influence of these superstars, and dozens of others, has transformed popular music throughout the world. The sounds of American pop can be heard in Egyptian hip hop, Iranian heavy metal, German rock, Japanese bluegrass, South African country and western, and Chinese "boy bands." As Starr and Waterman point out, pop music lovers in other nations relate to the "recurring themes of American popular music—love and sex, home and travel, materialism and morality, optimism and despair."[2]

With its broad range of cultural diversity, the United States remains uniquely suited to produce innovative sounds and styles that drive the modern pop music industry. A musical style originally sold on scratchy wax records in the early twentieth century now flies across the Internet at the speed of light. And through popular song, the musical story of America resonates with billions of listeners throughout the world.

CHAPTER 1

Musical Tales of American Life

The lyrics of almost every pop song tell a story. The tale may be a clear declaration of love, a humorous yarn, or a collection of images evoked by poetic lyrics. Whether the lyrics are direct or vague, the storytelling foundation of American pop music can be traced back to those who wrote and performed on the earliest popular records.

In the early 1900s the United States was a cultural mosaic of people from many different ethnic and racial backgrounds. People in various minority groups had tastes, styles, and experiences that were largely misunderstood in a nation largely ruled by white Protestant males. As a result, these groups were cast as outsiders and often faced discrimination, isolation, poverty, and homesickness. This social situation gave rise to the unique music styles developed among African Americans, poor Southerners, and Jewish immigrants from eastern Europe. The singers, songwriters, and musicians among the cultural outsiders had many stories to tell and they were able to find expression in music. In doing so, the composers created song styles that crossed social barriers while weaving their hopes, dreams, and worries into the cultural fabric of the nation.

Tin Pan Alley, a stretch of West Twenty-Eighth Street in New York City, was home to several music publishing companies that wrote some of the first pop music during the early 1900s.

Tin Pan Alley

There was no better place to hear the musical expressions of minority and immigrant groups than New York City. Between 1890 and 1910, about five thousand European immigrants a day passed through the federal immigration center on Ellis Island in New York Harbor. About 2.5 million of these immigrants were Jews fleeing violent anti-Semitism in Poland, Russia, and other eastern European nations. About 1 million settled in New York City, making it the most populous Jewish community in the world. Some of the most famous singers, songwriters, and performers of the early twentieth century had roots in New York's crowded, poverty-stricken Jewish neighborhoods.

As the most populous city in America at the time, New York was the nation's entertainment capital and its theaters were legendary. The city was also the business center for theatrical booking, music publishing, recording, and, after 1922, radio broadcasting. The heart of New York's music industry was a short stretch of West Twenty-Eighth Street between Broadway and Sixth Avenue. The street was densely packed with old office buildings filled with composers trying to write hit songs on cheap, upright pianos. The clattering sound of the pianos playing all at once sounded like pots and pans banging together and gave the street its nickname: Tin Pan Alley.

Tin Pan Alley was home to professional composers who wrote some of the earliest and most influential pop music. They produced hundreds of songs such as "In the Good Old Summertime," "Give My Regards to Broadway," and "Shine on Harvest Moon." These songs were known as standards because they were familiar to everyone and part of the standard repertoire for musicians across the country.

Several of Tin Pan Alley's most revered tunesmiths were the sons of poor Jewish immigrants. Composer and lyricist Irving Berlin was born near Belarus, Russia, in 1888 and grew up on New York's Lower East Side after his family settled there in 1893. Berlin began his career as a singing waiter, but found overnight success in 1911 by writing "Alexander's Ragtime Band." The recording of the song by singer Arthur Collins was the best-selling record for ten weeks and "Alexander's Ragtime Band" was recorded in later years by hundreds of popular artists.

In the sixty years that followed his first hit, Berlin went on to write dozens of legendary songs, including "Blue Skies," "There's No Business Like Show Business," and "God Bless America." Berlin's "White Christmas," first recorded by singer Bing Crosby in 1942, is one of the best-selling records of all time, with sales of more than 50 million. Later recordings of "White Christmas" by other artists sold an additional 120 million records.

There were many other classics written by Jewish American composers during the golden age of Tin Pan Alley that dated from the 1920s through 1930s. These hits included

The Dizzying Sounds of Ragtime

Hundreds of ragtime songs were recorded between 1905 and 1917, when the style began to fall out of favor. The old ragtime songs have a comically rigid rhythm that sounds dated by modern standards. During the ragtime era, however, people were so unaccustomed to the ragged rhythms that they were physically affected. Larry Starr, a professor of music, and Christopher Waterman, a professor of arts and culture, explain:

> [For] most white Americans, who had little experience dancing to syncopated music, ragtime pieces apparently created a slightly disorienting or dizzying sensation. Descriptions of the time stress the titillating effects of offbeat rhythms, sometimes likening them to a pinch of pepper used to spice up an otherwise bland soup or stew. Of course, it is important to remember that the [white] dancers' prior experience and cultural values conditioned these attributions of "spiciness." It seems likely that many African Americans would have found the mildly syncopated music performed by the most successful dance orchestras of the era neither stimulating nor scandalous.

Larry Starr and Christopher Waterman, *American Popular Music from Minstrelsy to MTV*. New York: Oxford University Press, 2003, p. 45.

Irving Caesar's "Tea For Two" and "Swanee," George Gershwin's "I Got Rhythm," and Jack Yellen's "Ain't She Sweet" and "Happy Days Are Here Again."

While the songs of Tin Pan Alley may sound old-fashioned to modern ears, they established rules for pop music that continue to influence songwriters. Tin Pan Alley composers used specific song themes based on beautiful women, romantic love, heartbreak, patriotism, and home and family. The lyrics were simple and the melodies memorable. Like many pop songs of later decades, Tin Pan Alley hits had sixteen measures, or bars, for each verse. Almost every song starts with a brief instrumental introduction, called a hook, that helps listeners instantly identify the song. A verse is sung that explains the subject matter of the song. This is followed by a refrain, or chorus, that is repeated after every verse.

Most Tin Pan Alley songs—and most pop songs today—have three verse-chorus sections. Some have an extra part called a bridge after the second chorus. The bridge has a different melody and rhythm than the rest of the song and provides a contrast to the repetitive verse-chorus pattern.

Powerful, Danceable Beats

The songs of Tin Pan Alley were light and happy, written to appeal to the broadest record-buying audience of their time, that is, white Americans who made up more than 85 percent of the U.S. population. Although black people were a minority, representing only 10 percent of the populace at the time, African American composers had great influence on early popular music. These musicians created three distinct styles of music, all of which have roots in West African rhythms. Black singers and songwriters from the delta region in western Mississippi invented the blues. African American musicians in New Orleans, Louisiana, created jazz, while skilled black piano players throughout the country pioneered ragtime.

Early blues, jazz, and ragtime songs were built upon ancient rhythms brought to the United States by African slaves. African-style rhythms feature several independent drumbeats that weave together in a mix called cross-rhythm or polyrhythm. This mix of different rhythms creates a powerful, danceable beat called syncopation.

Ragtime, developed by African American pianists in the late 1890s, is one of the earliest popular American musical genres based on syncopation. The style was originally called ragged time because the syncopated notes fell slightly ahead of—or behind—the strict succession of beats as written on sheet music.

A ragtime piano player tickles the keys, lightly playing a rhythmic melody while improvising licks with the right hand. The pianist uses the left hand to play a strong bass line to a slightly different beat, which creates the syncopation. This overall effect makes listeners want to dance.

Missouri-born Scott Joplin was the king of ragtime, and his 1899 composition "Maple Leaf Rag" created one of the first popular musical sensations. In this era before the widespread use of phonographs and records, the sheet music of "Maple Leaf Rag" sold more than 7 million copies.

The sheet music of Scott Joplin's "Maple Leaf Rag," which was written in 1899, sold more than 7 million copies.

Phonographs and Records

When Thomas Edison invented the phonograph in 1877, he could only imagine one purpose for the machine that reproduced sounds on wax-coated cylinders. Edison figured the recording device could be used by businessmen who wanted to dictate letters. Others, however, saw musical possibilities for the phonograph. As music historian Karl Hagstrom Miller explains, the phonograph, for the first time, "separated the voice from the body and enabled music to travel independently of musicians."

Around 1903, the first 12-inch (33.5cm) disc music records were sold. Unlike Edison's fragile wax cylinders, disc records were much more durable because they were made with shellac, a compound derived from rubber-eating beetles. Early disc records played at 78 rpm (revolutions per minute) and could hold about four minutes of music. In 1904 the double-sided disc was introduced so that two songs could be included on each record.

The Victor Talking Machine Company released a record by the famous Italian opera singer Enrico Caruso in 1904. Caruso was an instant hit and his 1907 recording of "Vesti la giubba" was the first to sell a million copies. Caruso went on to make 290 records for Victor before his death in 1921. By this time, Americans were buying more than 100 million records by various artists every year.

Karl Hagstrom Miller. *Segregated Sound*. Durham, NC: Duke University Press, 2010, p. 3.

Singing the Blues

In addition to syncopation, another musical feature of traditional West African music—the call-response technique—is found in early blues music. It is based on a lead singer calling out words, which others repeat in unison. The call-response technique, traditionally sung by Africans during religious ceremonies, was Americanized by black slaves picking cotton, building roads, and laying railroad tracks. The workers sang call-response songs called blues hollers. These simple songs were shouted out to distract workers from their harsh labors, while helping them perform difficult tasks in unison.

Blues hollers grew into a distinct musical style simply called the blues. Blues lyrics are a reflection of the painful experiences African Americans faced through slavery and discrimination and are associated with sadness, lost love, sickness, poverty, loneliness, and hopelessness. Music journalist Kevin Phinney describes the basic ideas behind the blues:

> [Blues composers] consider life to be a hardship in which every man, woman, and child is an orphan and anyone (including the narrator) is potential victim and culprit. With cautions that range from world weary to enraged, the blues . . . singer simply states what is: they're beaten down by bosses, betrayed by lovers, swindled by friends, at the mercy of the bottle, or dodging the law. . . . [To] have the blues diagnoses the victim as depressed and downhearted but singing [the blues] offers release, rejecting sorrow . . . in hopes of a brighter future.[3]

Each verse of a blues song has twelve bars, so the style is referred to as the twelve-bar blues. Blues songs were originally played by soloists on guitars or a four-string African instrument called the *banjar*, forerunner to the modern banjo. Blues singers often accompanied themselves with a harmonica hung on a rack around the neck. Various emotions, such as sadness, anger, and passion, were expressed through blue notes, in which the voice or the string of an instrument wavers between two notes. Players also improvised, using groups of notes to create melodies, or licks, that did not follow any written musical score. All this musicianship provided listeners with an edgy, moody, unpredictable musical experience.

Blues Royalty and Race Records

Most early blues artists were itinerant players, or traveling musicians, who wandered the South performing on street

corners and in rundown bars. Few white Americans ever heard the blues until Mamie Smith turned the blues into pop music. Smith was already a well-known Broadway performer when in 1920 she recorded "Crazy Blues" on the OKeh label. Smith was the first African American woman to make a record, and "Crazy Blues" sold seventy-five thousand copies within a month.

Smith's "Crazy Blues" is much more sophisticated than a guitar-driven blues song. The arrangement features clarinets, a slide trombone, and Smith's high, clear vocals that were obviously polished on the Broadway stage. While Smith's version of "Crazy Blues" sounds like a typical pop song of the day, the words are drenched in the blues. Smith

"Crazy Blues" singer Mamie Smith, center, the first African American woman to make a record, is surrounded by members of her band in 1920.

sings that she can't sleep at night because her man is gone. If she can't get him back, she's going to need an undertaker because she is being driven to the grave by the crazy blues.

"Crazy Blues" eventually sold well over a million copies and proved that music by African American singers could be extremely profitable for record companies. Within a year, OKeh achieved great success with blues records by black musicians Lonnie Johnson and Sippie Wallace.

Bessie Smith Shouts the Blues

One record company in particular was rescued by an African American blues singer. Columbia Records was nearly bankrupt, but was saved by Bessie Smith (no relation to Mamie), whose records outsold all others of the day. Smith's 1923 recording of "Down Hearted Blues," a twelve-bar blues song featuring her strong, unwavering vocals accompanied only by a piano, sold a remarkable 780,000 copies in six months. In the song, the singer describes how she has been mistreated, heartbroken, and disgusted by every man she ever met except her father and brother. Her life is wrecked and her only solace is in a jug of whiskey.

Bessie Smith was known as the Empress of the Blues. In 1967 renowned Harlem author Langston Hughes recalled that Smith was also referred to as a blues shouter: "Bessie did not attempt to entertain. She simply stood still and shouted the blues without trick arrangements or orchestral refinements—and she rocked the joint. Before the days of microphones, Bessie could be heard for a mile."[4]

The records made by Mamie Smith and Bessie Smith and other African American artists were called race records, because they were recorded specifically for black audiences. Race records became popular among young white music fans because they too could relate to stories of being broke, low-down, and brokenhearted. When whites took an interest in the blues, every major record company in America set out to create its own race record label to cater to this new market. Black composers, singers, and musicians who had been working in theaters and dance halls for years were suddenly a hot commodity.

Race records provided black artists entry into the music industry, but racist business practices ensured that few African Americans would profit significantly from the trend. While white singers and composers were paid a royalty, which is a percentage of every dollar made on a record, black artists were paid only a meager $50 to $250 per record. With the popularity of race records, royalty contracts could have made some black musicians wealthy.

The Jazz of New Orleans

The blues propelled race music to the top of music charts and provided an important foundation for jazz, which proved to be even more popular. Jazz music originated in the bars and bordellos of New Orleans around 1900. The term *jazz* comes from an African American slang word that means making love. Jazz or *jass* came to be used in the musical context to mean speed up the beat, or play with more intensity.

Early jazz was like the popular New Orleans stew called gumbo, which blended many different styles of foods, such as meat, shellfish, and a variety of vegetables, into one tasty dish. A traditional jazz music gumbo starts with a twelve-bar blues format, adds ragtime syncopation and West African polyrhythm, and layers on the brassy sounds of a marching band. The result is a music phenomenon called New Orleans, or traditional, jazz.

Traditional jazz is characterized by collective improvisation, in which every member in a band of musicians adds his or her own embellishments to the musical score. The music is also called polyphonic, meaning "many sounds," because every musician plays intently at the same time.

Each instrument has a specific role in a traditional jazz band. The coronet player carries the main melody while improvising licks to fill in between musical phrases. The clarinetist plays a countermelody, weaving a unique set of notes around the coronet. The trombone is a versatile instrument that allows players to add bluesy bass notes or a simple countermelody. One of the most exciting sounds elicited from the trombone is the slide, called the tailgate, in which the player creates blues notes by sliding from one note to the next, up and down the musical scale.

The Jazz Craze

Although jazz is an African American invention, the Original Dixieland Jazz Band (ODJB), made up of white musicians, created the first jazz-fueled pop music sensation. In 1917 the ODJB, led by Italian American coronet player Nick La Rocca, played at New York's esteemed Reisenweber's Restaurant. The syncopated dance sound alienated customers at first, but the band was soon drawing huge crowds. Talent scouts at Victor Records saw the lines to enter Reisenweber's stretching around the block and signed the ODJB to make a record, "Livery Stable Blues."

The Original Dixieland Jazz Band recorded the first jazz record, "Livery Stable Blues," in 1917, and started a pop music jazz fad.

The Original Dixieland Jazz Band's "Livery Stable Blues" was the first jazz record ever recorded. When it was released in March of 1917, the record sold 250,000 copies within months—at 75 cents a record—and went on to sell a million copies. It became the best-selling record in history at that time, kick-

ing off a jazz fad that would propel the pop music business for a decade.

The instant popularity of Dixieland jazz in the north prompted a mass exodus of jazz musicians from New Orleans. While some moved to New York, many moved to Chicago, Illinois, which became a booming center for black jazz. By the mid-1920s, some of New Orleans' hottest musicians were playing in Chicago's dance halls, including coronet player Joe "King" Oliver, clarinetist Sidney Bechet, and trombonist Edward "Kid" Ory.

Satchmo and His Hot Bands

Jazz took a great leap forward in 1922 when New Orleans native Louis Armstrong arrived in Chicago with nothing but an old trumpet and a torn tuxedo in a battered suitcase. Although Armstrong was only twenty-one years old, he had no musical equal in New Orleans. He could hit the highest notes with graceful ease and his skills at improvisation were already legendary.

Armstrong began his career at the age of thirteen, playing in New Orleans bordellos. His cheeks puffed out so much when he blew his horn that his mouth seemed as big as a large bag, or satchel. Before Armstrong was twenty, he was given the nickname Satchmo (Satchelmouth), and it stuck with him for the rest of his life.

In Chicago, Armstrong joined Joe Oliver's Creole Jazz Band and was an immediate hit. In an era known as the Jazz Age, he was the most critically acclaimed musician playing jazz. Armstrong recorded race records under his own name from 1925 to 1928, and with his Hot Bands of five or seven players, called the Hot Five or Hot Seven.

Armstrong's recorded work during the Hot Bands era still amazes jazz fans, and the records, which sold millions of copies, are considered masterpieces. The Hot Bands records feature extended solos by Armstrong and the other musicians, who are introduced by name on the song "Gut Bucket Blues." Armstrong also pioneered a new singing style when he dropped his lyric sheet during the 1926 recording of "Heebie Jeebies." Rather than stop the music, Armstrong sang a series of nonsensical words meant to imitate the snarling sounds of a trumpet. This technique came to be known as scat singing, and was widely imitated by other pop singers in later years.

Armstrong elevated the role of the soloist in a band and the popularity of polyphonic traditional jazz faded away. In the decades to come, nearly every pop record would have one or more featured soloists whose hot riffs helped drive the musical sound.

Fiddlin' John's Hillbilly Music

After record label OKeh made a fortune producing race records, the company's producer and talent scout, Ralph Peer, began searching for the next pop music miracle. He found it in Fiddlin' John Carson, who was often heard on Georgia radio stations. Peer considered Carson's singing so bad he had to make up a term to describe it: "pluperfect awful."[5] Whatever Peer's opinion, Fiddlin' John's 1923 recording of "The Old Hen Cackled and the Rooster's Going to Crow," with "Little Old Log Cabin in the Lane," on the flip side of the 2-sided record sold more than five hundred thousand copies. In the decade that followed, Fiddlin' John Carson went on to sell millions of records. His singing and fiddling style was treasured by working-class white Southerners. The music reminded listeners of their rural roots during an era of industrial expansion, when many were forced to leave their farms and log cabins to work in cotton mills and clothing factories.

Carson's style came to be known as hillbilly music, a term first coined by OKeh in the early 1920s. Although some found the term *hillbilly* demeaning because it described poor, undereducated rural people, it was widely used. Hillbilly music was originally called old time, or country music made by string bands. A string band might consist of a singing guitarist, mandolin and banjo players, a fiddler, and, occasionally, a pianist. String band rhythm could be provided by someone blowing into a whiskey jug or thumping on a washtub bass made of an old washtub, a protruding broom pole, and a rope strung tight between the two.

The Singing Brakeman

Carson's success paved the way for one of the most popular country singers in history. Jimmie Rodgers was born in a tiny town in the Mississippi Delta in 1897. As a young man, he learned to play music by listening to black bluesmen and local Choctaw and Natchez Indians who developed a vocal technique that is akin to yodeling. When Native Americans sang their traditional songs, they rapidly alternated notes between a normal singing tone and a high falsetto sound. Although yodeling is closely associated with Swiss mountain climbers, Rodgers developed what he called the blue yodel by listening to Native Americans.

The Singing Brakeman

In 1927 Rodgers traveled to New York City, where he recorded several songs for Victor Records. The song "Blue Yodel," also known as "T for Texas," sold five hundred thousand copies in months. This made Rodgers the best-selling artist on the Victor label.

Jimmie Rodgers, known as the Singing Brakeman and the Father of Country Music, recorded several popular songs in the late 1920s and early 1930s.

Before his success in music, Rodgers had supported himself by working as a brakeman on railroad trains, and many of his songs were about traveling on trains. This earned him the nickname the Singing Brakeman. Newspapers loved to write about the colorful Singing Brakeman. He was widely seen in photos, dressed in his railroad cap and denim jacket and holding his guitar.

Rodgers wrote dozens of hit songs that are now country standards. He quickly became a major celebrity and was billed on concert posters as "The Father of Country Music." His career, however, was cut short in 1933 when he died from tuberculosis. He was buried in the small town of Meridian, Mississippi, and the inscription on his gravestone reads: "His is the music of America. He sang the songs of the people he loved, of a young nation growing strong. His was an America of glistening rails, thundering boxcars, and rain-swept night, of lonesome pines, great mountains, and a high blue sky."[6]

Jazz Gets Sophisticated

Duke Ellington, center, and his orchestra perform in Los Angeles, California, in the 1930s. Ellington performed live on a weekly national radio broadcast from 1927 to 1933, showcasing his original compositions.

In growing urban areas like New York City, a new form of sophisticated jazz music was embraced by radio programmers who broadcast the sounds across the nation. Composer and pianist Duke Ellington pioneered the new sound. In 1927 Ellington formed the ten-piece Cotton Club Orchestra, which mixed the brassy sounds of traditional jazz with woodwinds and strings. The result was lush orchestral arrangements that were defined as sophisticated jazz.

Between 1927 and 1933, live concerts by Ellington and his orchestra were broadcast on national radio stations every Saturday night. This exposure propelled Ellington's music to the top of the pop charts and during this period he made more than 150 records of original compositions. Many of these songs, such as "Mood Indigo," "Sophisticated

Popular Music and Popular Culture

American pop music consists of songs that are shared by the entire nation. The emergence of this song style occurred in the 1920s, when technological advances in radio and film created a unified popular culture for the first time.

Radio experienced the fastest growth of any new medium. While there were only 3 radio networks in 1920, there were 564 in 1922. Within five years, national broadcasters such as NBC and CBS carried live broadcasts of popular singers and dance bands and also played records. This allowed listeners in New York, New York; Chicago, Illinois; Los Angeles, California; Seattle, Washington; Dallas, Texas; and everywhere in between to hear the same music.

Pop music got another boost in 1927 when the first movies with sound were produced. In the decades that followed, movies were a prime driver of pop music trends. For example, in 1939 actress Judy Garland sang the song "Over the Rainbow" in the film *The Wizard of Oz*. The song became a pop hit and helped make Garland a musical star.

In this new media milieu, pop entertainers were famous from coast to coast. This development brought millions of dollars to the entertainment industry and laid the foundation for the movie and record business as it is known today.

Lady," and "Take the A Train," are today considered jazz classics and are famous throughout the world.

Ellington's big band sound evolved into swing, which became the defining musical sound of the 1940s and World War II. Swing jazz was written and arranged by renowned bandleaders like Benny Goodman, Fletcher Henderson, Artie Shaw, Count Basie, and Glenn Miller. The big bands had twelve to twenty musicians, whose instruments fit into four divisions: a saxophone section, a reed or clarinet section, a trombone section, and a trumpet section. Drummers drove the syncopated beat and the rest of the band was filled out with piano, bass, and guitar.

Most swing bands had vocalists who would sing a few songs throughout the evening. Some of the most famous pop singers during the first half of the twentieth century started their careers singing with swing bands. These stars include Frank Sinatra, Ella Fitzgerald, Tony Bennett, and Billie Holiday.

A Continuing Influence

The musical genres developed during the first decades of the twentieth century—Tin Pan Alley, ragtime, blues, jazz, hillbilly, and swing—influenced pop music throughout the century and continue to do so. Aspects of these pioneering styles can be heard in nearly every pop song, from early rock and roll by Little Richard to later hits by the Rolling Stones, Michael Jackson, Madonna, and Justin Timberlake. Without the styles developed in the 1910s, 1920s, 1930s, and 1940s, American pop music as it is known today would not be the same.

CHAPTER 2

Rockin' Around the Clock

In the early 1950s the music industry trade magazine *Billboard* tracked weekly sales figures of popular songs on a chart known as the hit parade. In this era, before rock and roll, pop music was dominated by slow, romantic ballads made by adults, for adults. Musical arrangements featured syrupy violins, swirling woodwinds, and pianos. Drums were not played on these records—the weak rhythms were kept by the soft thump of the stand-up bass. Fifties record producer Arnold Shaw writes, "Big fiddle-faddle orchestras . . . played lush mood music for relaxing, cocktails, and vacationing in far-away places."[7]

Early fifties hit parade songs were often recycled from earlier decades. The song "Yellow Rose of Texas" by orchestra leader Mitch Miller was written in the 1830s. Singer Eddie Fisher's "Oh My Papa" was a nostalgic German song from the 1930s. Other big sellers were silly novelty songs such as "How Much is that Doggie in the Window?" and "If I Knew You Were Comin' (I'd've Baked a Cake)."

One of the few interesting developments in the music industry at this time was a new type of vinyl record that replaced poor-quality 78 rpm (revolutions per minute) records which held about 3 minutes of music per side. The new records had a higher quality sound and were unbreakable. Singles, which played at 45 rpm, held one 3- to 4-minute

The Shrinking Record

New technology in radio and records drove popular music sales in the first half of the twentieth century, and this remained true during the rock era. The record revolution began in June 1948 when Ed Wallerstein, chairman of Columbia Records, held a press conference at the prestigious Waldorf Astoria Hotel in New York City. Wallerstein directed the reporters' attention to an 8-foot-high (2.4m) stack of 78 rpm (revolutions per minute) records on one side of the stage and a 15-inch-high (38.1cm) pile of 33⅓ rpm records on other side. Wallerstein gestured dramatically at the smaller pile and pointed out that the 33⅓ rpm, or LP (long playing), records, held as much music as the towering pile of old-fashioned shellacked 78s. In ad-

dition, the 33⅓s were made from a relatively new material, vinyl plastic, which was virtually indestructible.

Vinyl records had a much better sound than 78s, which contained cracks, clicks, and scratches that were often louder than the music. The new records were also available in stereo, with right and left channels that allowed instruments and voices to be separated on the recording. Perhaps the most revolutionary change in records in the late 1940s was the introduction of the 45 rpm single. Most pop singles in the following decades had one song on the "A side" that was chosen as a possible hit, while the flip side, or "B side," held a song by the same artist that was deemed less commercial.

song on each side. Long-playing (LP) records, which played at 33⅓ rpm, could be up to 50 minutes in length and hold six songs on each side.

White Man Singin' the Blues

The most innovative music produced by white artists in the early fifties was on *Billboard*'s country-and-western (C&W) charts. A new style, called honky-tonk music, captured the rowdy feel of roadside bars, where hardworking men and women drank cheap beer and danced on Saturday nights. A typical honky-tonk band consisted of a singing guitarist, a fiddle player, a drummer, a bass player, and a guitarist who used a metal bar to create a vibrating, sliding guitar sound on a laptop or pedal steel guitar.

Honky-tonk singer Hank Williams had eleven songs top the charts in the late 1940s and early 1950s.

Most honky-tonk songs are based on a twelve-bar blues format and feature lyrics about cheating lovers, absent spouses, and the joys and sorrows of drinking. Because of the similarity to the blues, honky-tonk music was called the "white man's blues"[8] by country superstar Merle Haggard.

The hit songs by hillbilly singer Hank Williams catalog a typical honky-tonk litany of the blues: "I'm So Lonesome I Could Cry," "My Son Calls Another Man Daddy," "I Just

Don't Like This Kind of Livin,'" and "Your Cheatin' Heart." Williams wrote hundreds of songs and had eleven number one hits in the late forties and early fifties. Many of his songs were autobiographical. His wife cheated on him, his marriage was turbulent, and it ended in divorce. Williams was also addicted to morphine, prescription drugs, and alcohol. This combination killed him at the age of 29, on New Year's Day 1953, in the back of a car on his way to a show in Canton, Ohio.

During the early fifties, other honky-tonkers, like Lefty Frizzell, Hank Snow, George Jones, and Earnest Tubbs, were pioneers of the white man's blues. The honky-tonk music they created influenced a generation of rock-and-roll musicians.

Rhythm and Blues and Big Business

While the honky-tonk musicians adapted blues to fit their own circumstances, traditional African American blues was moving in an entirely different direction. *Billboard* began listing African American hits in the "Race Records" chart in 1945, and in 1949 the chart was given a new title, "Rhythm and Blues (R&B) Records." While few outside the record industry noticed the name change, as music journalist Donald Clarke writes, "the strands of black pop had come together. The blues had come to town, and rhythm and blues was big business."[9]

The term *rhythm and blues* was coined by renowned Atlantic Records producer Jerry Wexler when he was a young record reviewer at *Billboard* in 1948. Wexler found the term *race* objectionable, so he used rhythm and blues for the style of music that mixed urban-based jazz with the twelve-bar blues form, backed by a heavy, driving beat.

The original R&B style can be traced to the jazz combos in the late forties that featured a guitar, stand-up bass, piano, drums, and a horn section with a strong saxophonist. This style featured syncopation in which the drummer highlighted the second and fourth beats, or backbeats, in each four-beat measure. Songs with a strong backbeat make people want to dance. When hot, improvised solos by individual players and blues-like lyrics are shouted over the music, a song has both rhythm and blues.

King of the Moondoggers

In 1951 Leo Mintz, who owned one of Cleveland, Ohio's biggest record stores, noticed that his white teenage customers were buying R&B records. Some of the most popular black artists were Bullmoose Jackson, Peppermint Harris, and Eddie "Cleanhead" Vinson. It was easy to see the appeal of this music to young people raised on the innocuous hit parade. Many of the songs were about taboo subjects with sly and often humorous lyrics about drinking, fighting, and loving. Jackson's "I Know Who Threw the Whiskey in the Well" and "I Want a Bowlegged Woman" are typical of this style sometimes called dirty blues. The lyrics are risqué and the music is driven by a fast-paced, swinging boogie-woogie piano, hand claps, and honking saxophone.

Mintz was friends with Alan Freed, a Cleveland disc jockey (DJ) who spent his evenings playing classical music on WJW radio. Mintz introduced Freed to R&B music, saying "the beat is so strong that anyone can dance to it without a lesson."[10] Mintz persuaded Freed to host a new R&B radio show after midnight, and in June 1951 *The Moondog Show* went on the air. Pop music critic Ed Ward describes Freed's outrageous style, which had never been heard before on radio:

Todd Rhode's "Blues for Moondog," a wailing sax solo, would start things off, with Freed's mike open, howling like a demented coyote, then he'd slide into the program with his patented gravelly voice. . . . He kept a thick Cleveland phone book within easy reach, not far from his ever-present bottle [of Scotch] and over a particularly wild saxophone instrumental, he'd begin beating the rhythm out on the phone book, wailing "Go! Go! Gogogogogogogo! Go! Go!" It was crazy, it was close to anarchy. It was just what a very large number of teenagers had been waiting all their lives to hear.[11]

Rocking and Rolling a Baby Boom

The post–World War II baby boom included children as young as 9 years old, teenagers, and those in their early 20s. White members of this unique cultural group were the most prosperous in American history. They were the first generation raised on television, the first to grow up in suburbs, and the first to rock and roll. Music critic Robert Palmer recalls the impact of hearing rock music on Alan Freed's late-night radio show:

> [We were huddled] under bedroom covers with our ears glued to a radio pulling in black voices charged with intense emotions and propelled by a wildly kinetic rhythm through the after-midnight static. Growing up in the white-bread America of the Fifties, we had never heard anything like it, but we reacted . . . instantaneously and were converted. We were believers before we knew what it was that had so spectacularly ripped the dull, familiar fabric of our lives. . . . We found out they called it rock & roll. It was so much more vital and alive than any music we had ever heard before that it needed a new category: Rock & roll was much more than a new music for us. It was an obsession and a way of life.

Quoted in Holly George-Warren, ed. *Rolling Stone: The Decades of Rock & Roll.* San Francisco: Chronicle Books, 2001, p. 13.

Freed began calling the R&B songs he played rock and roll. This slang word for sex had been used by African American singers as long ago as 1922, when Trixie Smith sang "My Man Rocks Me (With One Steady Roll)." In the late 1940s rocking and rolling was mentioned by dozens of R&B artists, who sang lyrics such as "I rock 'em, roll 'em all night long"; "there's gonna be good rockin' tonight"; and "all she wants to do is rock."

A Rock-and-Roll Anthem

Freed's biggest fans were members of the postwar generation known as the baby boomers. The baby boom was a surge in population that began in 1945, after the end of World War II, when veterans returned home, married, and started families. It lasted about twenty years, and during this period more than 77 million babies were born in the United States. By 1958 there were 19 million teenagers in America, and by the mid-1960s more than 40 percent of all Americans were under the age of twenty. Throughout the 1950s, baby boomers developed their own teen culture, which was spread to every village, town, and city by rock-and-roll music.

If American teenagers liked a song, they went out and bought it with their allowances. This could make any song a best-selling pop phenomenon overnight. No one understood this better than Bill Haley, who started his career in the 1940s as the "Rambling Yodeler" in a C&W band called the Saddlemen. Like many country singers, Haley loved the blues and boogie-woogie music. In 1953 the Saddlemen changed their band's name to Bill Haley & His Comets to record the song "Crazy Man, Crazy."

Haley based the song's title and lyrics like "go, go, go" and "man that's really gone" on teenage slang he heard when his band played at high school dances. Musically, "Crazy Man, Crazy" combines a boogie-woogie bass beat with a honky-tonk guitar sound, all played in a twelve-bar blues format. This hybrid of white and black music styles came to define rock-and-roll music throughout the 1950s. It also propelled "Crazy Man, Crazy" to number twelve on the *Billboard* hit parade, making it the first rock-and-roll song to become a pop hit. When "Crazy Man, Crazy" was used on the "Glory in the Flower" episode of the 1953 CBS television show *Omnibus*, it was the first rock song ever played on TV.

Haley's biggest success, "(We're Gonna) Rock Around the Clock" (now known simply as "Rock Around the Clock"), became a rock-and-roll anthem in 1955. Ironically, the lyrics were not written by a boogie-woogie bluesman, but by a sixty-three-year-old music industry veteran, Max Freeman, previously known for his 1945 hit parade novelty song "Sioux City Sue."

Bill Haley (top) & His Comets recorded "Crazy Man, Crazy" in 1953, the first rock and roll song to become a pop hit. Two years later, the group had another hit with "(We're Gonna) Rock Around the Clock."

When Haley initially recorded "Rock Around the Clock" in 1954, it was a moderate hit. One year later, however, when the song blasted out loudly over the opening credits of the film *Blackboard Jungle*, it caused a sensation. *Blackboard Jungle* was about a group of rebellious juvenile delinquents in an inner-city school who smash their teacher's prized collection of 78 rpm jazz records. In several cities throughout the United States and Europe, the movie brought out rowdy mobs of teenagers who frightened adults by singing, pounding on seats, and throwing popcorn. There were even minor riots in several cities. "Rock Around the Clock" was rereleased and quickly sold 6 million copies, making it the best-selling record in history at that time. Music journalist Fred Bronson explains that the song was more than just a hit: "It was a signal flare, warning that all that followed would be different from all that came before."[12]

The Sun Shines in Memphis

Haley's music might have been a warning signal, but no one was prepared for the musical explosion that was catching fire in Memphis, Tennessee. Located north of the delta on the Mississippi River, Memphis was at the crossroads of musical culture in the early 1950s. Blues players from the delta and jazz bands from New Orleans played the nightclubs that catered to an African American clientele on the city's famed Beale Street.

Memphis also attracted white musicians from across the South. Some cut records at Sun Studios, founded by recording engineer Sam Phillips and his assistant Marion Keisker. In the early 1950s Phillips struggled to earn a living making records by delta guitar wizards such as B.B. King and Howlin' Wolf, who would go on to become blues legends in later years. To make ends meet, Sun allowed amateur musicians into the studios to make records for their families and friends. One such customer, a poor eighteen-year-old truck driver named Elvis Presley from Tupelo, Mississippi, entered the studio with his guitar in July 1953. He paid Keisker $3.25 plus tax to record two songs for his mother's birthday.

Phillips paid little attention to Presley, but Keisker took notice of his unique singing style. Meanwhile, Phillips continued to face financial problems because white radio stations would not play the African American music he was recording. Phillips told Keisker he needed to discover a white country boy who could sing R&B songs: "If I could find a white man with the Negro sound and the Negro feel, I could make a million dollars."[13] Keisker suggested Presley and Phillips called him into the studio.

Elvis Is All Shook Up

In a June 1954 recording session, Presley recorded the blues song "That's All Right" by Arthur "Big Boy" Crudup, an African American bluesman. Crudup's 1946 recording featured lyrics that were shouted out over driving drums, a swinging guitar, and walking bass line. Presley's version, with studio musicians Scotty Moore on guitar, Bill Black on

stand-up bass, and no drums, sounded like a fast-tempo country song.

Presley also recorded a rocking version of the country waltz "Blue Moon of Kentucky" to back the single. Phillips quickly understood he had found his "white man with the Negro sound." Music historian James L. Dickerson explains, "With 'That's All Right' they took a blues song and spun it white. With 'Blue Moon of Kentucky' they took a white song and spun it black."[14]

Much of this musical style had to do with Presley's amazing voice, described by music professor Richard Middleton as "swooping almost two octaves at times, changing timbre from a croon to a growl instantaneously . . . sometimes within the course of a single phrase."[15] "That's All Right" became a regional Memphis hit when it was played repeatedly on C&W radio stations.

Presley was at first marketed as "The Hillbilly Cat," but he was not a country-and-western cowboy. With his satin jacket, pompadour hairdo, long sideburns, and pelvis-shaking dance moves, Presley drove teenage girls wild. The singer's popularity attracted the attention of RCA Records, the biggest record company in America, which bought his contract from Phillips in November 1955. Phillips continued to produce innovative new artists, including country singer Johnny Cash and rockers Roy Orbison and Jerry Lee Lewis.

On January 27, 1956, RCA released Presley's emotion-charged "Heartbreak Hotel." The next day, Presley appeared on national television for the first time. He sang "Heartbreak Hotel" on a program called *Stage Show*. On April 6, when Presley sang the song on *The Milton Berle Show*, an estimated one-quarter of America's teenage population was watching. By this time, *Billboard*'s pop music chart was called the Hot 100. "Heartbreak Hotel" was number one for eight weeks and went on to become the best-selling single of 1956. This was Presley's first gold record, a designation for records that sold more than five hundred thousand copies.

Presley quickly became a pop sensation. Girls swooned

Elvis Presley sings and performs his hip-shaking dance moves on stage in front of a mob of screaming teenage girls in 1956.

over his singing, while boys picked up guitars and began styling their hair into pompadours. This created a media backlash. When Presley appeared on *The Ed Sullivan Show*, he was shown only from the waist up because his dancing was considered too sensuous for television. *Time* magazine described Presley's famous dance move as "a frantic quiver, as if he had swallowed a jackhammer."[16]

Whatever the complaints of his critics, by the end of 1956, *Billboard* reported Presley had charted more songs than any other artist in the history of the magazine. Combined sales of his singles "Hound Dog," "Don't Be Cruel," "Jailhouse Rock," "All Shook Up," and "Love Me Tender" reached fifty thousand copies a day. Many of these early singles were backed by the strong, driving rhythm of drummer J.D. Fontana, while Bill Black slapped the strings of his stand-up bass. This sound came to be known as rockabilly, or African American rock performed by hillbilly musicians.

Rockabilly Madness

In a 1986 interview, Sam Phillips said, "Elvis had a certain type of total charisma that was just almost untouchable by any other human that I know of or have ever seen."[17] Phillips also noted the piano-pounding Jerry Lee Lewis was the most talented person he ever worked with, black or white.

Lewis's 1957 singles "Whole Lotta Shakin'" and "Great Balls of Fire" went straight to the top of *Billboard*'s C&W and R&B charts while hitting number two on the pop charts. His antics, onstage and off, earned him the nickname "Killer." When Lewis performed, he abused his grand piano, climbing on top of it to sing or pounding the keys with his feet. On one occasion he lit an expensive, hand-crafted piano on fire.

While Lewis set the tone for wild rock-and-roll performers for years to come, his rock career was short-lived. In 1958 the British press discovered the twenty-three-year-old Killer had married his thirteen-year-old cousin. The scandal derailed Lewis's career for more than a decade and he never achieved the level of stardom as when he first recorded for Sun Studios.

Rip It Up

By combining black and white musical styles, rockabilly and rock and roll broke down the strict racial barriers that governed society, especially in the South during the 1950s. For decades, black patrons at music venues were forced to sit in the balconies while white patrons were seated on the main floor. When rock performers came to town, this practice ended. The music was so wild, black and white teens danced together.

Rock and Roll Brings the Races Together

Little Richard was one of the first rockers to break down the walls of segregation in the mid-1950s by playing to both black and white audiences. He recalled those days for his biographer Charles White:

We were breaking through the racial barrier. The white kids had to hide my records 'cos they daren't let their parents know they had them in the house. We decided that my image should be crazy and way-out so that the adults would think I was harmless. I'd appear at one show dressed as the Queen of England and in the next as the pope.

They were exciting times. The fans would go really wild. Nearly every place we went, the people got unruly. They'd want to get to me and tear my clothes off. It would be standing-room-only crowds and 90 percent of the audience would be white. I've always thought that Rock 'n' Roll brought the races together. Although I was black, the fans didn't care. I used to feel good about that. Especially being from the South, where you see the barriers, having all these people who we thought hated us, showing all this *love*.

Quoted in David Brackett, ed. *The Pop, Rock, and Soul Reader*. New York: Oxford University Press, 2005, p. 93.

"Little Richard" Penniman, a black pianist and singer born in 1932 in Macon, Georgia, was one of the first rockers to break through the racial barrier, playing to integrated audiences in the mid-1950s. Little Richard claims to have invented rock and roll and points to his songs "Tutti Frutti," "Rip It Up," and "Good Golly Miss Molly" to support that claim. Incorporating the opening line of "Tutti Frutti," Donald Clarke describes Little Richard's style:

> [The] inmates had left the asylum, never to be recaptured, with a cry of WOMP-BOMP-A-LOO-MOMP ALOP-BOMP-BOMP! Little Richard was bisexual, he wore make-up, he was a tornado on stage and he passionately shouted dirty songs. . . . In two minutes Richard Wayne Penniman used as much energy as an all-night party.[18]

While Little Richard certainly helped invent rock and roll, his wild piano pounding, intense screams, and sexually charged singing style made him too hot for the hit parade. Instead, he found his greatest success on the pop charts in the 1950s when Elvis Presley and bland balladeer Pat Boone recorded toned-down versions of "Tutti Frutti" and some of his other songs.

Rocking the Electric Guitar

The rock-and-roll guitar innovator Chuck Berry, an African American, wrote songs for white audiences because, as he told a *Rolling Stone* reporter in 2001, he set out to make a million dollars when he began his career in music and there was more money in the white music market. White people made up 90 percent of the record-buying public, or as Berry put it, "nine pennies out of every dime."[19]

Berry is known as the first rock-and-roll poet, because the clever wordplay in his lyrics went far beyond the typical hit parade songs of the day. His first hit, "Maybelline," based on the 1930s country song "Ida Red," tells the humorous

---

Pianist and singer Little Richard Penniman, known for his wild playing and screaming voice, was one of the first rockers to play to integrated audiences in the mid-1950s.

Chuck Berry's songs featured clever lyrics and hot guitar licks that made him popular among teenagers in the mid-1950s.

story of a man in an inexpensive Ford chasing his girl-friend Maybelline as she drives with another man in his big Cadillac. Tunes such as "School Days (Ring! Ring! Goes the Bell)" and "Sweet Little Sixteen" were aimed directly at teenagers in the suburbs. "Johnny B. Goode," "Rock and Roll Music," and "Roll Over Beethoven" were the first to celebrate rock and roll as an essential need in life.

When Berry ripped into his hits, he often hammered out a hot lick on his Gibson guitar unaccompanied by any band members. This instantly elevated the role of electric guitars to lead instruments in rock. In later years, the famous open-ing lick from "Johnny B. Goode" was imitated by dozens of pop guitarists.

Buddy Holly, from Lubbock, Texas, helped make another type of guitar famous. Holly's Fender Stratocaster, or Strat, gave a bright, sharp sound to his 1958 rockabilly hits like "That'll Be the Day," "Rave On," "Oh, Boy," and "Peggy Sue." When Holly appeared on the scene with his distinctive eyeglasses and his Strat hanging around his neck, he became an instant rock icon. Holly's songs have been covered by dozens of pop artists since the late 1950s and have come to define the rockabilly era of pop music.

"Authentic Artists Were Destroyed"

Buddy Holly's career was cut tragically short. On February 3, 1959, he was killed in a small plane crash in Iowa along with Hispanic pop star Ritchie Valens and novelty songwriter J.P. "the Big Bopper" Richardson. This marked the end of the initial phase of rock and roll, which lasted little more than five years. By the time of Holly's death, almost all of rock's founders were missing from the scene. Some, like Jerry Lee Lewis, were sidelined by personal problems, while others were hurt by authorities who set out to neutralize the most rebellious creators of the music.

Alan Freed's career was ruined by a congressional investigation that revealed he engaged in a common, but illegal, practice called payola, which is taking money from record companies to play specific records. In 1959 Chuck Berry was arrested on allegations that he transported a minor across state lines for immoral purposes. Berry maintained his innocence but spent eighteen months in jail as his career foundered. Meanwhile Elvis Presley had been drafted into the U.S. Army in 1958, disappearing completely from the music scene for the next two years. Commenting on this era, *Rolling Stone* magazine music critic Robert Palmer writes, "[Rock and roll's] takeover of the pop-music marketplace in the mid-Fifties was as threatening to the entrenched old-line music and entertainment business as it was to professional authority figures everywhere."[20]

By 1960, old-line pop producers were sanitizing rock and roll, promoting teen idols like Frankie Avalon, Paul Anka, and Bobby Darin, who did not shout or growl out the lyrics

By the early 1960s, pop crooners including (from left) Paul Anka, Bobby Darin, Frankie Avalon, and Pat Boone became teen idols at the center of a wave of "sanitized" rock and roll.

but crooned them sweetly. Commenting on this phenomenon, notable Cleveland disc jockey Bill Randle noted in *Billboard*'s December 1958 issue, "I think tastes have changed. . . . Rock and roll is being integrated into popular music. It's no longer a novelty. Rock and roll was an earthy, virile influence, but the authentic artists were destroyed."[21] As the 1960s dawned, rock and roll was being written off as a temporary pop fad and millions of parents and authority figures were glad to see it go. They had no idea what the next decade would bring.

CHAPTER 3

The Sixties Sound Explosion

In the 1960s pop music exploded into many different subgenres. The *Billboard* charts were topped by acoustic folk music, sweet harmony songs, electric rock bands, and an updated R&B style called soul. By the late sixties these styles had been woven together in numerous combinations such as folk rock, country rock, blues rock, and psychedelic pop masterpieces that defied classification.

Unlike the rock-and-roll revolutionaries of the 1950s, most sixties chart toppers did not emanate from the South. Singer-songwriter Bob Dylan hailed from Minnesota; rock bands like the Beatles and Rolling Stones were British; the Beach Boys played surf music from Southern California; guitar wizard Jimi Hendrix grew up in Seattle, Washington; and the hottest soul music on the air came from Detroit, Michigan. This geographical spread shows that rock and roll had achieved an amazing influence far beyond its Southern roots. Most sixties superstars, however, were strongly influenced by rock's 1950s founding fathers.

In 1959 Dylan wrote in his high school yearbook that his ambition was "to join Little Richard,"[22] that is, to play in his band. Hendrix actually did play in Little Richard's band in 1964, and soon began imitating Richard's flamboyant style of dress. Two years later, just as he was becoming famous,

The Beach Boys' Good Vibrations

In the 1960s California was idealized in films and on TV shows as a carefree, sun-kissed place where summer never ended. In the world of pop music, no one generated better musical imagery of surf, sand, and sunshine than the Beach Boys. The group was a family affair, composed of the Wilson brothers Brian on bass and keyboards, Carl on guitar, and Dennis playing drums. They were joined by their cousin Mike Love on lead vocals and their friend Al Jardine on guitar. Together, the group charted fifty-six songs in the Hot 100, and had four number-one hits.

The music produced by the Beach Boys between 1962 and 1965 reads like entries in a typical teenager's diary in Southern California: "In My Room," "Surfin'," "California Girls," "Be True to Your School," "Fun, Fun, Fun," and "I Get Around." The songs had rocking guitars reminiscent of Chuck Berry and complex harmonies and smooth, vocal arrangements unlike any other group. In 1966 the Beach Boys released their biggest hit, "Good Vibrations," a three-minute, thirty-five-second song with so many layers of instruments and voices that it took six months to produce and employed fourteen extra studio musicians. In the twenty-first century, Beach Boys songs remain staples on oldies radio stations and continue to evoke an age of sun-splashed innocence from long ago.

Hendrix told a reporter, "I want to do with my guitar what Little Richard does with his voice."[23]

Southern American music also had a major influence on British teenagers. When Beatles founder and guitarist John Lennon was growing up in Liverpool, England, in the early 1950s, he listened to country and western, blues, and R&B on the radio. When he heard Elvis Presley singing "Heartbreak Hotel" on the radio in 1956, he decided to become a rock-and-roll musician. Lennon later explained the pull of his early musical influences: "Rock'n'roll was *real*, everything else was unreal. . . . I had no idea about doing music as a way of life until rock'n'roll hit me."[24]

Breaking Down Gender Barriers

There is little doubt that some of the biggest names in 1960s pop were inspired by the first generation of rock and rollers, but these new stars were baby boomers. They had different experiences and expectations, and this was especially true for young women. In the United States in the early 1960s, women were attending college in record numbers. The invention of the birth control pill meant, for the first time, women could experience more sexual freedom without fear of pregnancy.

Sexism and traditional gender discrimination remained in place throughout society in the 1960s, however. Women did not have equal rights to men even though they were playing larger roles in many areas, including the pop music business. This was obvious to those who worked in the Brill Building, an eleven-story office building in New York City.

Husband-and-wife duo Gerry Goffin, left, and Carole King were among several Brill Building songwriters who penned hit pop songs in the late 1950s and early 1960s.

Home to more than 160 music businesses that created, published, recorded, and promoted pop music, the Brill Building was a modernized version of Tin Pan Alley. The songwriters and record producers who worked in the building catered to the needs of millions of teenage baby boomers by creating memorable dance music and songs about love and broken hearts.

Although the music business had long been dominated by men, in this new era, three of the most celebrated Brill Building tunesmiths were young women. Carole King, Cynthia Weil, and Ellie Greenwich were married to their writing partners, Gerry Goffin, Barry Mann, and Jeff Barry, respectively. Many of the songs written by the husband-wife teams of the Brill Building were number one hits recorded by "girl groups," which comprised both black singers and white singers.

It was the Goffin-King song "Will You Love Me Tomorrow?" that launched the girl group industry in January 1961. The song was recorded by four young African American women, who had formed a group called the Shirelles several years earlier when they were in junior high school. King was barely out of high school herself, just 18 when she wrote the lyrics to "Will You Love Me Tomorrow?" about her ex-boyfriend. After the first hit by the Shirelles, Goffin-King hits dominated pop radio. The duo composed songs about dance crazes, like Little Eva's "Loco-motion" and girl group classics about love and longing like the Chiffons' "One Fine Day."

Motor City Soul

The Brill Building was not the only hit factory in early sixties America. In Detroit, African American songwriter Berry Gordy Jr. founded the Motown Record Corporation in 1959. Gordy assembled teams of songwriters, producers, musicians, singers, and record promoters who labored in a small bungalow marked only by a sign that said "HITSVILLE, U.S.A." The motto of Motown was "the sound of young America,"[25] because Gordy's goal was to reach all teenagers, of all races.

Some of Motown's biggest early hits were written and produced by the songwriting brothers Brian and Eddie Holland, who teamed up with Lamont Dozier. These men, known as Holland-Dozier-Holland, came to define the Motown sound, writing and producing songs with popping rhythms, catchy hooks, soulful lead singers, and soaring background harmonies.

The songs of Holland-Dozier-Holland were the driving force behind the Motown girl group success of the Supremes, composed of singers Florence Ballard, Mary Wilson, and Diana Ross. The Supremes, who grew up together in the same Detroit housing project, went on to become one of the best-selling pop groups of the 1960s. In total, the Supremes sold more than 100 million records. Their hits included "You Can't Hurry Love," "Baby Love," "Come See About Me," "Stop! In The Name of Love," and "You Keep Me Hanging On." Holland-Dozier-Holland also wrote a string of soul hits for other Motown superstars, including the Four Tops ("Baby I Need Your Loving," "I Can't

Florence Ballard, left, Mary Wilson, and Diana Ross made up the Supremes, who had a string of pop hits for Motown Records in the 1960s.

Help Myself," and "Reach Out I'll Be There") and Marvin Gaye ("Can I Get a Witness" and "How Sweet It Is To Be Loved By You").

Smokey Robinson was another talent at Motown. He wrote pop hits for the Temptations like "My Girl" and a string of number one songs, including "You've Really Got a Hold on Me" and "The Tracks of My Tears," for his own band, the Miracles. Robinson sang in a soulful falsetto, and his songs explored romance, love, and heartbreak with clever turns of phrase. The lyrics to songs like "When the Hunter Gets Captured by the Game" and "Tears of a Clown" led Bob Dylan to call Robinson "America's greatest living poet."[26]

Between 1961 and 1971, Motown had 110 top ten hits written by Robinson, Holland-Dozier-Holland, Marvin Gaye, and others. Nearly every song started with a great dance beat, what Gordy called "that funk . . . that groove,"[27] followed by a memorable musical hook. To get into that groove, Gordy said, "We would try anything to get a unique percussion sound: two blocks of wood slapped together, striking mallets on little glass ashtrays, shaking jars of dried peas . . . a whole group of people stomping on the floor."[28]

The Beatles Pop Music Masterpieces

Motown hits might have been the sound of young America, but they were heard around the world. In 1962 the Beatles, a bar band in Liverpool, England, played live sets of Robinson's "You've Really Got a Hold on Me," as well as Brill Building girl group hits such as "Chains," "Boys," and "Baby It's You," and rock-and-roll classics by Little Richard, Chuck Berry, and Buddy Holly. The group, made up of guitarist John Lennon, bassist Paul McCartney, lead guitarist George Harrison, and drummer Ringo Starr, had learned to sing sweet, high harmonies covering Motown and other American pop songs.

The Beatles also wrote their own songs, and their catchy tunes made them major pop stars in England in early 1963. By December they had a number one hit in the United States with "I Want To Hold Your Hand," which went platinum, selling more than a million copies in a few days. This set off a fad called Beatlemania, a term invented by the press to describe the intense adoration the Beatles inspired in their fans.

When the group made their first American TV appearance, on *The Ed Sullivan Show* on February 9, 1964, about half the country—some 73 million Americans—watched. As John, Paul, George, and Ringo shook their long, shaggy hair and sang "She loves you, yeah, yeah, yeah," TV cameras showed teenage girls shrieking hysterically in the audience. By April, the Beatles had surpassed Elvis Presley's record-setting sales achievements. The top five *Billboard* hit songs were all by the Beatles and the group had fourteen singles in the Hot 100.

Lennon and McCartney were the primary songwriters for the Beatles and they rarely composed songs based on the twelve-bar blues form typical in rock music. Instead,

The Beatles make their first television appearance in the United States in February 1964, performing on The Ed Sullivan Show *before an audience of 73 million viewers.*

their songs were built on complex chord patterns played on the guitar with seventh chords used for a blues feel, minor chords used to create a moody sound, and jazz chords inserted to add a unique harmony. Their melodies ascend to high points that excite the listener, and their lyrics often use clever or humorous wordplay like "please please me" or "a hard day's night."

The Beatles never repeated their musical accomplishments from album to album. Each LP was sure to be a surprise, sounding completely different than the one before. Within the first three years of their success, they released seven albums containing enduring hits such as "Yesterday," "Ticket to Ride," "We Can Work It Out," and "Nowhere Man." In the mid-1960s almost everyone under the age of thirty in the Western world could sing along to these three-minute pop music masterpieces.

The Beatles let their creativity run wild in the recording studio, where they employed string quartets, the Indian sitar, and French horns, instruments never before heard in rock music. Along with their brilliant producer George Martin, the group invented new sounds by tinkering with tape recorders and other electronic gadgets.

Social and Musical Revolutions

The Beatles were the first British pop group to have major success in the United States and their popularity caused a wave called the British Invasion. Suddenly, previously unknown British groups such as the Dave Clarke Five, Peter and Gordon, the Animals, and Herman's Hermits had number one hits in America. The Rolling Stones began their career as a British Invasion band, achieving their first success in 1965 with "(I Can't Get No) Satisfaction."

Around 1966, the British Invasion was replaced by another kind of revolution. America was in a period of social upheaval that became known as the counterculture or hippie movement. Millions of baby boomers began to question accepted beliefs in their own lives and those held by society at large. They adopted their own slang and fashions that included long hair on both men and women, tie-dyed shirts, blue jeans, and love beads. These young adults, including pop stars like the Beatles and Rolling Stones, began experimenting with marijuana and LSD (lysergic acid diethylamide or acid). LSD was at the root of the hippie counterculture. While most people took the drug for enjoyment, it caused some users to experience "bad trips" filled with paranoia and extreme anxiety. It also caused users to hear colors and see sounds, which provided profound musical inspiration for some musicians. As a result of this intense, drug-fueled examination, many hippies became antiwar, antiauthority, and critical of powerful corporations.

In February 1967 the Beatles released a single that was unmatched in pop history. John Lennon wrote "Strawberry Fields Forever" during a period when he was experimenting with LSD, and the song is a dreamlike kaleidoscopic trip of swirling sounds. Lennon and George Martin created the song with layers of cellos, keyboards, backward cymbals, and a multistringed Indian instrument called a *swarmandal*. "Strawberry Fields Forever" showed that the Beatles, who were the biggest pop stars in the world, were making music that was experimental, eclectic, and progressive—and beyond classification. The song proved to all listeners that pop music could be more than rock, blues, R&B, or soul.

A Decisive Moment in Pop Music

"Strawberry Fields Forever" was the warm-up for the Beatles' psychedelic LP, *Sgt. Pepper's Lonely Hearts Club Band*, released in June 1967. Kenneth Tynan, music critic of the respected *London Times*, said *Sgt. Pepper* was such a revolutionary, game-changing piece of music that the album represented a "decisive moment in the history of Western civilization."[29] While some might consider this statement overblown, the album undoubtedly changed the way pop music was produced and marketed.

Sgt. Pepper was one of the earliest concept albums, in which all of the songs were based on a single idea or theme. On this album, the idea was that John, Paul, George, and Ringo were no longer the Beatles, but instead members of the fictional music group Sgt. Pepper's Lonely Hearts Club

Sgt. Pepper's Lonely Hearts Club Band, *a concept album released by the Beatles in 1967, forever changed pop music with its innovative cover art, production style, and themes.*

Band. The album contained several exceptional psychedelic rock masterpieces like "Lucy In the Sky With Diamonds," "Being For the Benefit of Mr. Kite!" and "Day in the Life." The lyrics of Harrison's "Within You Without You" discuss deep spiritual and philosophical concepts, while the music is a hypnotic mix of Indian instruments, such as the multi-string sitar and the tabla drums.

The album cover of *Sgt. Pepper* is as unique as the music. The Beatles are surrounded by dozens of life-size cardboard cutouts of famous people including Bob Dylan, Communist philosopher Karl Marx, and actors James Dean, Marlon Brando, and Mae West. The lyrics are printed on the album, another first, so listeners could sing along.

Part of the Beatles' appeal was always that they were funny, down-to-earth guys who easily related to their fans. According to Larry Starr and Christopher Waterman, *Sgt. Pepper* took this concept to a new level:

> [The] album was constructed to invite listeners' participation in an implied community. The record is a clearly and cleverly organized performance that . . .

actually [addresses] its audience. The opening song, "Sgt. Pepper's Lonely Hearts Club Band," formally introduces the "show" to come and acknowledges the listeners with lines like "We hope you will enjoy the show." . . . It [positions] the rock album as the creator of an audience community.[30]

Sgt. Pepper sold 8 million copies upon release, remained on Billboard's album charts for four and a half years, and remains one of the best-selling albums of all time.

The record was evolutionary in another way. Before the album was released, the pop music business was driven by sales of 45 rpm singles. Sgt. Pepper showed that a piece of popular music could be longer than a three- to six-minute single and that a pop artist could create a musical masterpiece that filled an entire album. As a result, LP albums became the dominant method of marketing music in the aftermath of Sgt. Pepper.

Dylan's Hard Rain

Nearly every pop musician who has topped the charts since the 1960s will acknowledge a debt of gratitude to the Beatles. Many will also credit the influence of Bob Dylan, whose trajectory to stardom occurred during the middle of Beatlemania. Unlike the early Beatles, however, Dylan did not begin his career writing playful three-minute love songs for teenagers. Instead, he composed songs up to eleven minutes long that contained lyrics that were profoundly poetic, bitingly political, or even insulting, angry, and vengeful.

Dylan grew up in the small town of Hibbing, Minnesota, in the early 1950s, listening to Hank Williams, Elvis Presley, Little Richard, folksinger Woody Guthrie, and bluesmen like Charlie Patton. After he moved to New York City in 1961, Dylan made a name for himself writing songs about critical social problems.

The 1962 album The Freewheelin' Bob Dylan contains several songs labeled "protest music" by the press. "Blowin' in the Wind" poses questions about war, prejudice, and repression. The song was a major hit for the folk trio Peter, Paul and Mary, and became an anthem for the civil rights movement during the 1960s. Other songs on Freewheelin' are

Like a Rolling Stone

In 2004 Bob Dylan's "Like a Rolling Stone" was named the number one song in Rolling Stone magazine's list of "The 500 Greatest Songs of All Time." Unlike nearly every other pop song up until that time, the lyrics to "Like a Rolling Stone" were vengeful and venomous. The song is also more than six minutes long, released at a time when disc jockeys would not play anything longer than three minutes. Despite its unique character, "Like a Rolling Stone" changed pop music as rock singer Bruce Springsteen commented in 1988 when he inducted Dylan into the Rock and Roll Hall of Fame:

> The first time I heard ["Like a Rolling Stone"] I was in the car . . . and on came that snare shot that sounded like somebody'd kicked open the door to your mind. . . . The way that Elvis freed your body, Dylan freed your mind, and showed us that because the music was physical did not mean it was anti-intellect. He had the vision and talent to make a pop song so that it contained the whole world. He invented a new way a pop singer could sound, broke through the limitations of what a recording could achieve, and he changed the face of rock'n'roll for ever and ever.

Quoted in John Bauldie, ed. *Wanted Man: In Search of Bob Dylan*. New York: Penguin Books, 1992, pp. 191–192.

angry commentaries about current events. "A Hard Rain's A-Gonna Fall" is a prediction of an apocalyptic nuclear war between the United States and the Soviet Union, while "Masters of War" is a scathing attack on war profiteers.

Dylan rejected the protest singer label, telling music critic Nat Hentoff in 1965 that he only started writing antiwar songs "because I didn't see anybody else doing that kind of thing. Now a lot of people are doing finger-pointing songs."[31] Although the media continued to call Dylan a pro-

test singer, he stopped writing obviously political songs in 1964 after recording another sixties anthem, "The Times They Are A-Changin.'"

Going Electric

In 1965 Bob Dylan shocked his fans when he picked up a Stratocaster guitar and jammed with a full electric band at the Newport Folk Festival in Rhode Island. Some members of the audience booed and yelled catcalls as Dylan ripped into "Like a Rolling Stone," and the event has become part of

Singer and songwriter Bob Dylan brought complex lyrics and social relevance to the pop music scene with hits such as "Blowin' in the Wind" in the early 1960s.

sixties lore, still remembered as the day Dylan "went electric." Despite the reaction from folk fans, Dylan continued to write amazingly creative, poetic songs unlike any other in pop history, including "Positively 4th Street," "Just Like a Woman," and "Memphis Blues Again." These songs are included on four groundbreaking LPs recorded in only two years, between 1965 and 1966: *Bringing It All Back Home, Highway 61 Revisited*, and the double album *Blonde on Blonde*.

Backed by pianos, electric organs, cutting lead-guitar riffs, bass, and drums, Dylan's new style was dubbed folk rock by the press. He disavowed the folk rock label, but bands like the Byrds, Buffalo Springfield, the Lovin' Spoonful, Simon and Garfunkel, the Mamas and the Papas, and the Turtles were able to blend folk and rock into chart-topping pop masterpieces in the mid-sixties.

Psychedelic Rock

Dylan might have been the first to blend folk, rock, and blues into pop hits, but bands that grew out of the hippie scene were adding yet another dimension to music. In the second half of the sixties, young middle-class teenagers from across America were flocking to the Haight-Ashbury neighborhood in San Francisco, California, where an ongoing hippie celebration of peace, free love, and psychedelic drugs was taking place. Dozens of bands made up of mostly local musicians formed to play psychedelic or acid rock for these eager music fans. This style, best represented by the band the Grateful Dead, could blend folk, rock, jazz, blues, and country into a single twenty-five-minute free-form jam.

Two of the most famous psychedelic bands were fronted by women who broke society's gender stereotypes and were proud of it. Former model Grace Slick was the lead singer for Jefferson Airplane. Unlike the sweet Brill Building girl groups and polished Motown signers, Slick's acid-drenched

Janis Joplin's raw, soulful performances blended blues, R&B, and rock styles in a way that was unique among women singers in the late 1960s.

Experiencing Jimi Hendrix

Jimi Hendrix is remembered by many as the best guitar player in rock history. His band, the Jimi Hendrix Experience, burst onto the pop scene with the 1967 song "Purple Haze." With the song's first distorted notes and power chords, Hendrix single-handedly invented heavy metal music.

Hendrix only released three studio albums—*Are You Experienced*, *Axis: Bold as Love*, and *Electric Ladyland*—before his drug-related death in 1970. On these records Hendrix creatively employed sound-manipulation devices like the wah-wah pedal and the fuzz box while playing lightning-fast licks. When he ap-peared in the 1967 movie *Monterey Pop*, Hendrix played his Stratocaster with his teeth, then played it behind his head, and then lit the guitar on fire. When he played at the Woodstock music festival in 1969, Hendrix presented a heavy metal version of the "Star Spangled Banner." With screeching feedback and vibrating fingers, Hendrix used his guitar and amps to imitate the rocket's red glare and bombs bursting in air. With his musical mastery, Hendrix expanded the boundaries of the electric guitar, set an almost impossible standard for others to match, and permanently changed the way lead guitar was played.

vocals were commanding, dramatic, and almost operatic. Jefferson Airplane's 1967 "Somebody to Love" is a psychedelic rock anthem, with a driving beat, soaring harmonies, and heavy, distorted lead guitars. The group's number one 1967 hit "White Rabbit," based on Lewis Carroll's book *Alice's Adventures in Wonderland*, was among the first chart toppers with blatant drug references.

Janis Joplin, who fronted Big Brother & the Holding Company, was even more outrageous than Slick. Joplin shrieked, cried, rasped, and swayed with her eyes closed, singing blues, R&B, rock, and even Tin Pan Alley hits while swigging from a bottle of Southern Comfort. Big Brother's album *Cheap Thrills* reached number one on the album charts and showed a generation of young women that they too could be rock stars. Rock journalist Lucy O'Brien writes, "When Joplin stood on stage and screamed out [the song] 'Piece of My Heart,' there was a sense of megalithic rock being resung and reinterpreted through a woman's perspective."[32]

Jim Morrison's Revolt, Disorder, and Chaos

Most San Francisco bands celebrated psychedelic drugs, love, peace, and freedom, but down in Los Angeles, California, Jim Morrison, lead singer for The Doors, had a darker view of the world. Morrison was a poet, and his lyrics often touched on stark observations about spiritual and bodily death. He told the *New York Times* that his songs were "about revolt, disorder, chaos. . . . It seems to me to be the road to freedom—external revolt is a way to bring about internal freedom."[33]

Morrison formed The Doors in the summer of 1965 with keyboardist Ray Manzarek, drummer John Densmore, and guitarist Robby Krieger. The group attracted a huge following playing in Los Angeles clubs and became major pop stars in April 1967 when the song "Light My Fire" was released as the first single from their debut album *The Doors*. The song "Light My Fire," with lyrics about getting higher and setting the night on fire, set the tone for all Doors albums to follow.

Morrison's revolution was self-destructive. In concert he was often drunk and high on drugs. He stumbled, yelled, jumped, and fell on the stage as if shot. He insulted the audience, then urged them to incite revolution. These antics troubled authorities and by 1968 the group was banned from playing in most cities. However, The Doors continued to produce number one hits, including "Love Me Two Times," "Hello, I Love You," "Touch Me," "Love Her Madly," and "Riders on the Storm." Morrison's drug and alcohol abuse contributed to his death in July 1971, but fans continued to buy Doors music for decades. By 2011 the group had sold more than 90 million records worldwide.

A Decade of Hits

The Doors were among the dozens of creative geniuses who dominated the *Billboard* Hot 100 between 1964 and 1969.

During any given week, the Beatles were competing with the Rolling Stones, the Byrds, Bob Dylan, the Rascals, James Brown, and half a dozen Motown artists. Songs by these acts are played on the radio every day and continue to sell in the twenty-first century.

The Beatles broke up in 1970, but their music continued to top the pop charts. When the entire Beatles catalog was offered on the iTunes Store for the first time in November 2010, more than 2 million individual songs and 450,000 Beatles albums were downloaded within days.

Dylan, who turned seventy years old in 2011, not only continued to sell his thirty-four studio albums and thirteen live albums, but he also remained a popular concert artist. Dylan toured the world performing new songs, old songs, and his immortal classics such as "Blowin' in the Wind," "Mr. Tambourine Man," and "Like a Rolling Stone" to three generations of fans.

Sixties pop music remains popular today and sets standards by which most music is measured. American pop music would not sound the same without the second generation of rockers who rose to fame during that turbulent decade.

CHAPTER 4

Big Sounds, Big Business

In August 1969 half a million baby boomers descended on Bethel, New York, to attend the Woodstock Arts and Crafts Festival. The three-day Woodstock concert is considered by many as one of the high points of the sixties. Music was provided by some of the biggest rock bands and stars of the era, including the Who, Jefferson Airplane, the Grateful Dead, Janis Joplin, and Jimi Hendrix. Although the festival was marred by traffic gridlock, rain, mud, poor sound, and a lack of provisions, the crowd was nonviolent and cooperative. In popular culture, Woodstock quickly came to symbolize all that was good about the counter-culture, a "Woodstock Nation" based on peace, love, and liberation.

The dream of a Woodstock Nation proved to be short-lived. In April 1970 the Beatles broke up, in September Hendrix died from mixing pills and alcohol, and in October Joplin died from a heroin overdose. Jim Morrison of The Doors died of drug-induced heart failure in early 1971. For many, these deaths heralded the end of sixties optimism. As John Lennon sang on his first solo album, released in December 1970, "the dream is over."[34]

Even as the hippie era faded away, sixties fashions, slang, and music were used by advertisers to sell everything from blue jeans to automobiles. The Doors, Jefferson Airplane, the

The Music Industry Expands

In the early years of pop, the most innovative music was promoted by small, independent labels like Motown and Sun Records. During the 1970s, profits generated by pop music attracted the attention of executives at major media corporations. By 1973, the independent labels were largely gone, consumed by six major entertainment corporations: Columbia/CBS, RCA, MCA, Capitol-EMI, Polygram, and Warner. These companies controlled 90 percent of the record business, which generated $2 billion in profits. This figure was almost twice as much as movie industry profits in 1973 and three times more than professional sports.

Growth in the music business was fueled by a new way to sell music: prerecorded tapes. Eight-track and cassette tapes had been introduced in the 1960s, but by the mid-1970s, they accounted for only one-third of music sales in America. In order to listen to music in their cars, millions of baby boomers bought albums on tape that they already owned on vinyl. Propelled by this phenomenon, record company profits doubled to $4 billion by 1978. The explosion of FM radio stations also encouraged record sales. More than a thousand new FM radio stations were founded in the 1970s, most of them dedicated to playing pop music for baby boomers.

Beatles, and Hendrix may have been leading a revolution, but when the media adapted hippie traditions for mainstream consumption, the counterculture became pop culture.

The Woodstock Effect

The mainstream acceptance of sixties rock was eagerly embraced by record company executives, concert promoters, and some of the bands that played at Woodstock. Crosby, Stills, Nash & Young (CSN&Y) and Santana, new groups that were virtually unknown before the festival, were swept up in what was called the Woodstock effect. When their debut albums were released, they instantly sold several million copies. Whereas gold records set the standard of achievement in the fifties and sixties, post-Woodstock groups were suddenly selling platinum and multiplatinum records.

The Woodstock effect also made a mark on the concert business. In the sixties only the Beatles could fill sports stadiums. In the 1970s rock concerts moved from theaters with five to ten thousand seats to huge arenas where seventy-five thousand people could see rock's growing list of superstars. Media critic Marc Elliot writes, "Rock's social statements turned into financial ones, as big-name performers eagerly traded their self-worth for net worth."[35]

Middle-of-the-Road Music

The pop music business model was always based on the production of moneymaking hits, but the Woodstock effect raised record companies' sales expectations. As a result, they would not promote groups that sold less than a million records. In order to find out what would sell, record companies hired a new breed of professional analysts to study and dissect the tastes of the music-buying public. Customers were divided into categories, or demographics, based on age, race, geographical location, and financial circumstances. This led to record companies creating a host of new musical categories for each demographic, or segment of the population.

Baby boomers remained the largest music-consuming demographic, and by the mid-1970s, the first wave of boomers turned 30. Millions of people in this age group were married, buying homes, raising families, and becoming more politically conservative. Although aging boomers grew up listening to the rebellious rock of the fifties and sixties, their musical tastes were mellowing. Record companies responded to this trend by promoting laid-back ballads called middle-of-the-road music, or MOR.

The MOR style was exemplified by the Carpenters, a brother and sister vocal duo consisting of Karen and Richard Carpenter. Their run of number-one hits began with the

1970 song "(They Long to Be) Close to You," written by Brill Building veterans Hal David and Burt Bacharach. In the song, Karen's wholesome-sounding vocals are backed by mellow piano and violins, creating the feel of an early fifties hit parade tune.

The Carpenters produced a steady stream of soft-rock hits like "We've Only Just Begun" and "Rainy Days and Mondays." Their music was popular on FM radio stations that featured new formats variously labeled easy listening, adult contemporary, or soft rock. These interchangeable genres, invented by a professional radio consultant named Lee Abrams, defined music that was made by white artists. The soft songs about love and life featured acoustic

Richard Carpenter, left, and Karen Carpenter, whose hits were typical of middle-of-the-road music of the 1970s, take to the recording studio in 1972.

guitars, pianos, sugary string sections, and syrupy background vocals. Drums were toned down or nonexistent.

Many artists besides the Carpenters took advantage of the growing number of FM stations featuring soft rock, including singers Barbra Streisand and Neil Sedaka, and the vocal groups Tony Orlando & Dawn and the Captain & Tennille. One of the top-selling adult contemporary artists in the seventies was singer and piano player Barry Manilow. His 1974 song "Mandy" was the first of twenty-two consecutive Top 40 hits that included "I Write the Songs" and "Copacabana." Critics panned Manilow's sentimental soft-rock songs, which were considered so bland he was called Barry Mayonnaise. Despite the critics, Manilow's sales figures put him in the same category as some of rock's biggest stars. In 1978 he had five platinum albums on the charts at the same time, and by 1983 he had sold more than 40 million albums.

Personal and Emotional Songwriters

Although Manilow's songs were very popular among middle-class women, he did not compose his biggest hits.

The Sounds of Seventies Country

In the 1970s companies that advertised on the radio realized their best customers were white males between the ages of 18 and 34. Musically, this demographic could be divided by region. For example, album-oriented rock appealed to young men on the East Coast, while Southerners preferred country pop. In the mid-1970s country artists such as Kenny Rogers, John Denver, and Glen Campbell produced number-one country pop hits that featured acoustic guitars, violins, and steel guitars. Some of these songs, like Rogers' "The Gambler," Denver's "Thank God I'm a Country Boy," and Campbell's "Rhinestone Cowboy," were crossover hits, popular with both country and pop audiences.

Country fans with rowdier tastes popularized a style called outlaw country in the mid-seventies. The leading outlaws were Willie Nelson and Waylon Jennings, who sang boisterous honky-tonk music filled with electric guitars, fiddles, harmonicas, and mandolins. Outlaws had long hair, smoked marijuana, and rebelled against the clean-cut conservative image associated with traditional country music stars. Southern rock bands such as Lynyrd Skynyrd and the Marshall Tucker Band were an offshoot of the outlaw movement, providing slick guitar licks and a boogie beat to young fans of rock and country music.

Other soft rockers, known as singer-songwriters, wrote their own songs, which gave them musical credibility with fans and critics.

The seventies was the era of singer-songwriters and chart-topping artists such as Paul Simon, Jackson Browne, Jim Croce, James Taylor, Carly Simon, and Neil Young. These people composed songs that were deeply personal, while expressing emotions that most everyone could relate to. One of the most successful singer-songwriters, Carole King, wrote many hits in the early sixties when she worked as a Brill Building songwriter. In 1971 King emerged as a solo artist, singing and playing piano on the influential album *Tapestry*, which features the hits "I Feel the Earth Move," "It's Too Late," and "(You Make Me Feel Like) A Natural Woman." King's soulful and insightful songs appealed to female baby boomers, who were beginning to exert their independence. Larry Starr and Christopher Waterman explain:

> "It's Too Late" is clearly an *adult* relationship song, written from the point of view of someone who has left behind her teenage crushes, insecurity, and desperate heartbreak. The singer describes the ending stage of a significant relationship with a feeling of sadness, but also with a mature philosophical acceptance that people can change and grow apart.[36]

King's *Tapestry* was the biggest-selling album in history at the time, topping number one on *Billboard's* top LP list for six weeks and remaining on the charts for six years. The album sold more than 25 million copies worldwide.

Album-Oriented Stardust

While the adult contemporary genre catered to the oldest baby boomers, Lee Abrams developed the album-oriented rock (AOR) format to appeal to younger white audiences. The AOR format was inspired by counterculture FM radio disc jockeys in the 1960s, who played whatever songs they liked and thought the public should hear. Many of the tracks in this format, originally called free-form, were not singles but songs from LPs. Abrams formalized the AOR format by creating lists of songs DJs should play. While critics complained that this made FM radio bland and predictable, some of the biggest rock superstars of the 1970s achieved success without creating number-one singles. They sold millions of albums and filled stadiums because their music was played continually on album-oriented rock stations.

One of the early beneficiaries of AOR radio was an unlikely candidate for pop music stardom. In the early 1970s, when hippies dominated the airwaves, bisexual British singer David Bowie cultivated a glittery, androgynous look that incorporated aspects of both genders. He posed

David Bowie performs in 1973 as Ziggy Stardust, the main character from his concept album of the same name, which made him a star.

as 1930s movie star Marlene Dietrich on his 1971 album *Hunky Dory*. The following year, Bowie transformed himself into Ziggy Stardust, a fictional rock star who is part human, part space alien.

Ziggy's story is the basis for Bowie's concept album *The Rise and Fall of Ziggy Stardust and the Spiders from Mars*, often referred to as simply *Ziggy Stardust*. Ziggy comes to Earth for five years before the planet is to be destroyed. He comes as the "Starman," an alien who will save everyone. With his message of hope, Ziggy Stardust becomes a huge star, but he is destroyed by the trappings of fame, including drugs, sex, and his own fanatical followers.

Bowie not only invented Ziggy Stardust, but he also became the character onstage. He appeared in concert with bright orange hair and heavy face makeup, dressed in plastic platform boots and bizarre glittery jumpsuits. With such performances, Bowie cynically celebrated the theatrical excesses of crass pop commercialism, claiming that with Ziggy, "I packaged a totally credible plastic rock star."[37]

A Radio Star

Bowie's success can be traced to WMMS, an AOR radio station in Cleveland. The station's music programmer Denny Sanders and DJ Billy Bass were so impressed with *Ziggy Stardust*, they began playing songs from the album, as well as *Hunky Dory*, practically nonstop. This inspired Bowie to play his first American concert in Cleveland, and another concert two months later.

Bowie's success was apparent by the concert halls he played. During his September 1972 Cleveland concert, Bowie played a theater that held about three thousand people. In November he played the city's largest venue, Public Hall, for a sold-out show before twelve thousand people.

With the help of WMMS, Bowie started a trend called glitter rock, also called glamour or glam rock, that was based on showy, theatrical rock spectacle. Although *Ziggy Stardust* only peaked at number seventy-five on the *Billboard* album charts, Bowie's following albums, such as *Diamond Dogs* and *Young Americans*, reached the top ten. By this time Bowie had abandoned the Ziggy Stardust character in favor of the pasty and extremely skinny "Thin White Duke" image.

Whatever character Bowie was selling, he helped advance the popularity of glitter rock. This helped acts like Lou Reed, the New York Dolls, Alice Cooper, and Kiss achieve widespread popularity fueled by their androgynous appeal, outrageous costumes, and songs picked by AOR radio station programmers.

Led Zeppelin's Musical Thunder

The hard-rocking, hard-partying British band Led Zeppelin, formed in 1968, was another superstar rock act whose fame was driven by AOR radio. Led Zeppelin lead guitarist and songwriter Jimmy Page melded blues, psychedelic rock, and English folk music with the distortion-heavy, hard-rock style pioneered by Jimi Hendrix. On occasion, Page would take out a violin bow and drag it across his electric guitar strings, creating what *Rolling Stone* senior editor Timothy White calls "ear-hemorrhaging solos."[38]

Zeppelin lead singer and lyricist Robert Plant was also accused of making listeners' ears bleed when he screamed out lyrics with his high, tenor voice. Combined with the virtuoso musical thunder produced by bassist John Paul Jones and drummer John Bonham, Led Zeppelin set album sales records and filled stadiums from coast to coast during their annual concert tours.

Led Zeppelin served as a musical model of artistry and excess that came to symbolize bad-boy rock star behavior in the 1970s. Drugged, drunken band members partied with female fans, destroyed hotel rooms, threw televisions off balconies, and, on one occasion, drove a motorcycle through the hallways of the Hyatt House hotel in Hollywood, California.

The Heavy Metal Kids

Beyond their rock-and-roll antics, Led Zeppelin is best known for the perennial AOR hit "Stairway to Heaven," known by some as the anthem of heavy metal. The

eight-minute-long song, first released in 1971, joins two contradictory musical styles. It begins with Page fingerpicking a beautiful melody on the twelve-string acoustic guitar, while Plant softly sings poetic lyrics that evoke ancient mystical imagery. About halfway through the song, the drums enter and the heavy metal phase of the music begins with Plant screaming and Page wailing on an electric guitar. In an unusual arrangement for a rock song, the tempo increases from 72 beats per minute (bpm) to 98 bpm. As Larry Starr and Christopher Waterman describe it, "The recording can itself be seen as an analogue of the heavenly stairway, springing from the rural, mythological past . . . soaring on jet-powered wings of metal, and finally coming to rest on a high, peaceful plateau."[39]

The song "Stairway to Heaven" first appeared on the untitled album known as *Led Zeppelin IV*. Despite never having been released as a single, "Stairway to Heaven" was the most requested song on FM radio in the 1970s. Driven by the success of this song, Led Zeppelin went on to become the fourth best-selling musical act in history. The group sold more than 300 million records worldwide before it disbanded in 1980 with the alcohol-related death of Bonham.

Renowned rock critic Lester Bangs called Led Zeppelin the "Heavy Metal Kids"[40] in 1969. Today the group is credited with inventing heavy metal music, a rock style picked up by dozens of seventies supergroups including Black Sabbath and Deep Purple. Other AOR bands, including Journey, Foreigner, and Aerosmith, achieved success with a slightly less heavy hard-rock sound. Like Zeppelin, these bands featured lead singers with high, tenor voices, lead guitar players with lightning-fast fingers, and drummers whose pounding could rattle the teeth of audience members, even those sitting up high in the stadium cheap seats.

Guitarist Jimmy Page performs as part of Led Zeppelin, whose music blended elements of blues, psychedelia, and English folk music to create a unique brand of hard rock.

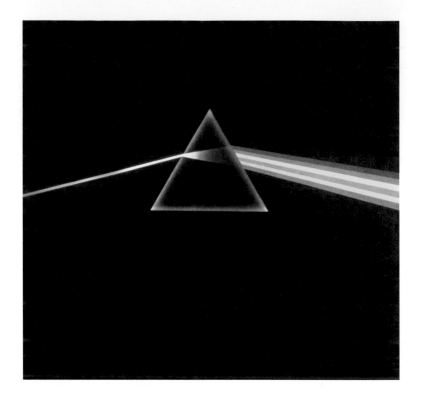

A prism centers the iconic cover of Pink Floyd's Dark Side of the Moon, *which remained on the album charts for 741 weeks, from 1973 to 1988.*

A Sonic Extravaganza

In the seventies Led Zeppelin was one of several British supergroups that dominated AOR radio and packed stadiums with screaming fans. Pink Floyd began playing psychedelic rock in London in the mid-1960s. The group's music could be playful, soothing, or, with songs like "Be Careful with the Ax Eugene," terrifying. Pink Floyd consisted of bassist Roger Waters, drummer Nick Mason, keyboardist Richard Wright, and guitarist Dave Gilmour.

According to music journalist Chris Smith, in the early seventies the members of Pink Floyd "were the lead astronauts in the universe of space-rock."[41] Their albums of the era, such as *Ummgagumma*, *Atom Heart Mother*, and *Meddle*, have simple, beautiful songs with acoustic guitars, as well as those with long, psychedelic jams and sound effects that might include frying bacon, squawking chipmunks, or buzzing flies. Gilmour's masterful Stratocaster solos could sound like spaceships landing or seagulls circling overhead.

Pink Floyd albums barely charted in the United States until the surprising breakthrough of their eighth album, *Dark Side of the Moon*. The lyrics, all written by Waters, are dark, pondering war, death, and insanity. Pop music journalists Scott Schinder and Andy Schwartz describe the groundbreaking album as a:

> painstakingly constructed sonic extravaganza. . . . a complete and cohesive artistic statement. . . . [that] featured state-of-the-art production, with an artfully layered sonic palette that incorporated inventive sound effects, spoken-word snippets . . . wailing backup vocals, and . . . uplifting saxophone work. . . . [The] album set new standards for the rock genre."[42]

Every song on *Dark Side of the Moon* was played on AOR radio, and the album went on to break all sales records. *Dark Side of the Moon* remained on *Billboard*'s top LP charts for 741 weeks (more than 14 years), from 1973 to 1988. By comparison, *Tapestry*, the second longest-selling album on the charts, was listed for 302 weeks, while the third runner-up, *Led Zeppelin IV*, was listed for 259 weeks.

Pink Floyd remained among the most successful bands of the era, following up *Dark Side of the Moon* with chart-topping albums like *Wish You Were Here*, *Animals*, and *The Wall*. Before they disbanded in 1983, the group sold more than 200 million albums.

Dreams of Fleetwood Mac

Fleetwood Mac is another British supergroup that started in the sixties and rose to prominence in the seventies. The group was originally formed by drummer Mick Fleetwood, bassist John McVie, and John's wife, keyboardist Christine McVie. The group found mainstream success in 1975 when they added two American songwriters, singer Stephanie "Stevie" Nicks and her boyfriend, guitarist Lindsey Buckingham.

With two female singers, Fleetwood Mac was popular among young women who related to the emotional pull of romantic songs like McVie's "Go Your Own Way" and "Don't Stop" and Nicks's "Rhiannon" and "Dreams." Before the band went on a hiatus in 1982, Fleetwood Mac produced a string of number-one hits that dominated FM radio. The group's 1977 *Rumours* sold more than 40 million copies and is one of the top ten best-selling albums in history.

The Eagles Take It Easy

The mellow country-rock sounds of the Eagles, with an early line up of (from left) Bernie Leadon, Glenn Frey, Don Henley, Randy Meisner, and Don Felder, dominated rock radio in the 1970s.

Like many singer-songwriters of the era, Fleetwood Mac had a laid-back, well-produced sound. However, no group better exemplifies the mellow 1970s sound than the Eagles. The band was formed in Los Angeles in 1971 by guitarists Glenn Frey and Bernie Leadon, bassist Randy Meisner, and drummer Don Henley.

The Eagles expertly synthesized country and rock music to produce songs that were loved by urban, suburban, and rural audiences. The group combined seamless high harmonies, twangy guitars, and a steady, driving pop beat. The Eagles released the compilation album *Their Greatest Hits (1971–1975)* in 1976, and it contained a body of songs that

were popular with many radio formats, including AOR, adult contemporary, and country. Every song on the album was a chart topper, including "Take It Easy," "Desperado," "Lyin' Eyes," and "Peaceful Easy Feeling." Leadon and Meisner left the band in 1976 and were replaced by Joe Walsh and Timothy B. Schmit respectively, but Henley and Frey continued to write number-one country rock hits like "Hotel California," "The Last Resort," and "Life in the Fast Lane."

The Eagles broke up in 1980, but re-formed in 1994, conducting periodic concert tours that were hugely successful. In 2011, after nearly forty years of producing peaceful, easy pop hits, the Eagles remain a constant fixture on radio stations throughout America.

Dancing to Disco

Most of the seventies supergroups created songs that prompted listeners to analyze their deep lyrics, unique chord progressions, and slick productions. What Pink Floyd, Fleetwood Mac, and the Eagles failed to do was make dance music. As renowned music journalist Mikal Gilmore writes, this left a gap that needed to be filled: "[There] were audiences for whom dancing was a vital social bond and an essential sensual act, though they were . . . shut out by rock & roll's developing styles and pretentions."[43] This vital need was filled by disco, a new genre that was one of the biggest pop music movements of the decade.

Disco music melds sixties soul, Latin music, and funk, a rhythmic style driven by a prominent bass line and an insistent syncopated drumbeat. Disco came to life in urban dance clubs that catered to African American, Hispanic, and gay customers. The pioneers were not musicians but disc jockeys who worked with two or three turntables, spinning short sequences of songs to create what Gilmore calls "a mounting mood of physical frenzy among the dancers."[44]

In the second half of the seventies, disco seemingly came out of nowhere to conquer pop culture. Stars like Gloria Gaynor, Donna Summer, Patti LaBelle, and KC and the Sunshine Band had number-one singles featuring the irre-

Disco Demolition Night

The success of the 1977 film *Saturday Night Fever* made disco the most popular music in America. This created an anti-disco movement promoted by some disc jockeys on album-oriented rock stations. The disco backlash made headlines in July 1979 when a Chicago, Illinois, disc jockey promised to blow up a crate of disco records at "Disco Demolition Night" at Comiskey Park before a White Sox baseball game. More than ninety thousand people showed up at the fifty-two-thousand-seat stadium for the event. Many had their own disco LPs to burn. Before long, thousands of hard-edged records were sailing through the stadium like Frisbees, wounding countless people. As the countdown to the disco demolition took place, the huge crowd began chanting "Disco sucks." When the records exploded into a fiery mass of burning plastic, thousands rushed onto the infield and a riot erupted. Many music fans viewed Disco Demolition Night as a shameful event. Disco producer Nile Rodgers, who went on to produce Madonna, compared the event to the Nazi book burnings of the 1930s. The disco fad was over by the early 1980s, even as the infectious disco beat was used in hundreds of mainstream pop hits.

sistible disco dance beat. The style proved to be so popular that other stars, such as the Rolling Stones, Barry Manilow, and even Pink Floyd, inserted the disco beat into their songs.

The 1977 film *Saturday Night Fever*, which portrayed disco nightlife as lived by urban youth, featured disco music by various artists, including sixties British rockers the Bee Gees, who reinvented themselves for a new era. More than any other record, the sound track album *Saturday Night Fever* brought disco to the mainstream. The LP was the number one album from January to July 1978, and stayed on *Billboard*'s album charts for 120 weeks, until March 1980.

While the disco beat was heard everywhere, the music fad died nearly as quickly as it started. By 1980, many mainstream music fans had grown tired of the predictable disco beat. Radio stations began advertising disco-free weekends and practically overnight the slogan "Disco sucks" began appearing everywhere on T-shirts and bumper stickers. As music critic Vince Aletti notes, "Disco became a dirty word."[45]

A Punk Backlash

Disco was not the only musical genre facing a violent backlash. The wealthy, pretentious superstars who dominated

The Ramones, including guitarist Johnny Ramone, left, and singer Joey Ramone, right, were among several punk bands that came on the rock scene in the 1970s.

the pop charts created a wave of hateful anger among a new generation of fans who were too young to remember the sixties. In New York City, bands like the Ramones and Television donned the leather jackets of 1950s rebels and invented punk rock. They pounded out simple, loud, two-minute-long songs on guitars while screaming angry lyrics about unemployment, hypocritical people, and other social problems. While punk rock never became mainstream music, several successful pop bands of the era, such as Blondie and the Talking Heads, began their careers as punks.

With the rise of punk rock, the seventies had come full circle. The decade began with the death of the rebellious counterculture and closed with the birth of punk insubordination. Between those two cultural bookends, the pop music industry became one of the most profitable businesses in the world. From Woodstock to glitter to punk, the musical winners were rewarded with fabulous fortunes and everlasting fame.

CHAPTER 5

Video Stars and Rock Rebels

The world of pop music changed forever on August 1, 1981, though few noticed at the time. At one minute after midnight, a new cable TV channel launched in northern New Jersey. It began with the words "Ladies and gentlemen, rock and roll,"[46] spoken on camera by John Lack, one of the channel's creators. Moments later a music video played, appropriately named *Video Killed the Radio Star*, by a British group called the Buggles. The video was a sign of things to come.

The attractive musicians with weird haircuts wore oversize sunglasses, mouthed the words to the song, and pretended to play their instruments as the scenes changed rapidly. A handheld camera jiggled, panned from left to right, and zoomed in and out. Jump cuts—very short clips of scenes shot from different angles—were spliced together to achieve a dizzying effect.

The fast-paced Buggles video was totally new. The cable channel was called Music Television, or MTV. The station ushered in a new era in pop music, one that continues more than three decades after the Buggles sang a silly song about the power of television.

Creating and Selling an Image

In the twenty-first century, it is taken for granted that pop stars will endorse just about any product and sell their music for commercials and movies. While frowned upon in the sixties and seventies, the trend towards extreme commercialism in rock music accelerated rapidly in the 1980s. *Rolling Stone* editor Anthony DeCurtis explains:

> To a greater degree than ever before, marketing—the creation and selling of an image—became an essential component of an artist's success. Videos, video compellations, long-form videos, corporate sponsorships, product endorsements, T-shirts, book deals, interviews, television appearances, movie tie-ins, songs for soundtracks—all that began to envelop what was once considered a rebel's world. . . . Being a rock & roll star became a *job*, and true to Eighties ethic, you'd better be willing to put in the hours and produce—to smile and make nice with the powers that be—or you might go back to [performing in] the bars. By the mid-Eighties, rock & roll was well on its way to becoming terminally safe. . . . [Artists] seemed eager to sell out, to lease their songs to sell products, to put their dreams in the service of commerce.

Quoted in Holly George-Warren, ed. *Rolling Stone: The Decades of Rock & Roll.* San Francisco: Chronicle Books, 2001, pp. 175–176.

Musical Videotapes

Only a few thousand people viewed the launch of MTV, but within two years the channel was available in most American cities and suburbs. The instant popularity of MTV was unprecedented and quickly began driving the record sales of bands shown in videos. In June 1983 even the serious news reporter Ted Koppel took notice, telling viewers MTV "has done wonders for a sagging record industry. It has made overnight stars of rock groups. . . . It uses some of the most creative visual and editing techniques seen on television. . . . [You] may not have yet seen it, musical video tapes . . . set to slick, sometimes bizarre, choreography. It's a bonanza for singers, dancers, musicians, and the record industry."[47]

The Second British Invasion

Most of the groups experiencing the MTV bonanza were from Great Britain, where the Beatles made the first film clips to promote their music in the 1960s. During MTV's first three years, videos by previously unknown British acts, such as Thomas Dolby, Duran Duran, and the Thompson Twins, were in constant rotation. Robert Christgau, who calls himself the "dean of American rock critics," derided these English bands as "appearance-obsessed art-school types . . . with their high-IQ haircuts and dumb hooks."[48] Despite the critics, the British bands on MTV became overnight pop stars. The band Flock of Seagulls is a good example of the MTV star-making machine. Music industry journalist Tom McGrath writes:

> Flock of Seagulls released their first American single, an echoey dance-rock track called "I Ran," in June [1982]. . . . Their synthesizer-heavy sound didn't

British new wave band Flock of Seagulls, including (from left) Ali Score, Paul Reynolds, Mike Score, and Frank Maudsley, became pop stars overnight because of their exposure on MTV in the early 1980s.

seem right for either album rock or Top-40 radio, and frankly, the band wasn't even popular in England. Still, they made an interesting video . . . and so during the summer the clip was added to MTV's playlist. Within weeks "I Ran" began rising up the charts, and radio stations, most of which had initially ignored the song, were following MTV's lead and adding the song to their rotations. By the end of the summer, "I Ran" was in *Billboard*'s Top 10 . . . and the Seagulls . . . were playing huge arenas around the country.[49]

Other British musical acts, including the Police, Eurhythmics, Culture Club, and Elvis Costello, became major stars on MTV in the early eighties. David Bowie, who had achieved success in the 1970s, was another Englishman whose videos, like *China Girl* and *Modern Love*, were in heavy rotation on MTV. In the music industry this phenomenon became known as the Second British Invasion (the First British Invasion having occurred in the 1960s when the success of the Beatles produced a flood of British bands coming to America).

The Second British Invasion was given a major boost in early 1983 on the recommendations of powerful radio consultant Lee Abrams. At the time, Abrams was under heavy criticism for turning AOR radio into a haven for older music or "dinosaur rock" from the late 1960s and the 1970s. Abrams reacted by inventing the "Superstars II" format to once again make radio a leading source of new music, or what he called the modern sound. Abrams advised his hundreds of clients at FM stations across the country to double the amount of modern-sound music they played. Most of the new songs came from MTV, which was creating new superstars virtually overnight. By mid-1983, half of the records on *Billboard*'s Top 40 chart were by British bands.

A New Thriller for MTV

MTV was designed to appeal to white suburban teenagers. For the first eighteen months of its existence, MTV refused to play clips by black artists like Rick James, whose album *Street Songs* had gone triple platinum. Facing charges of racism, the channel decided to air Michael Jackson's video of "Billie Jean" in April 1983. Jackson first sang with his brothers in the Jackson Five in 1964 when he was six years old. By the age of eleven, Michael Jackson was a pop star who sang lead on number-one Jackson Five hits including "ABC" and "The Love You Save."

Jackson recorded his first solo album in 1972 and was a major star by 1979, when his album *Off the Wall* sold more than 6 million copies. By the time his sixth solo album, *Thriller*, was released in November 1982, the twenty-four-year-old singer was a perfect fit for MTV. Jackson looked good, he could dance like no one else, and *Thriller* appealed to a broad demographic. The song "Beat It" had a funky dance beat that was popular in urban dance clubs. The gritty guitar solo on the song by hard-rock maestro Eddie Van Halen, of the rock group Van Halen, was tailored to attract white AOR fans. Another *Thriller* single, the mellow MOR ballad "The Girl Is Mine," features Jackson singing with Paul McCartney. The duet with a former Beatle attracted millions of older baby boomers to the record.

The popularity of Michael Jackson's "Billie Jean," a single from his 1982 album Thriller, *was boosted by its groundbreaking video, the first by an African American artist to be played in heavy rotation on MTV.*

Within a year of its release, *Thriller* sold more than 10 million copies in the United States alone and it would go on to sell more than 100 million, making it the best-selling album in history. Some of this success was driven by Jackson's video clips. *Billie Jean*, the first video by an African American artist to receive regular play on MTV, shows Jackson at his finest. He spins, jumps, and slides with a grace and style unmatched by any other dancer on MTV. Jackson's look was also new. His hair was loosely curled and he was dressed in a glittery black jacket, pink shirt, and red bowtie. Within weeks, students across America were imitating Jackson's look. Jackson's next video, *Beat It*, was even more popular. The video was directed by a Broadway choreographer and cost more than $150,000 to make. Tom McGrath writes,

The Synthesizer Keyboard

Electric guitars made the sound of rock and roll possible in the 1950s and expanded the range of pop music in the 1960s. In the 1980s the synthesizer keyboard played a role comparable to the electric guitar in previous decades. The Yamaha DX7, introduced in 1983, was the first commercially successful digital synthesizer. The electronic instrument can produce a wide range of sounds that imitate piano, organ, woodwinds, brass, strings, bass, and drums. Synthesizers can also be programmed to combine these sounds with unusual electronic effects unlike any produced by traditional instruments.

The list of artists using synthesizers is a who's who of eighties and nineties superstars. The instrument is featured heavily on Madonna's *Like a Virgin* and on Michael Jackson's *Thriller* and *Bad*. Synthesizers also drive the sound and beat of most British electronic dance and new-wave bands. The British electronic music group Depeche Mode, which has sold more than 100 million records worldwide, relied heavily on the synthesizer for its 1980s hits like "Everything Counts." By the mid-1980s, synthesizers were providing pop music composers and producers with a totally new vocabulary of sounds that simply could not have been created in an earlier decade.

"What made it great was the dancing. Michael, dressed in a red leather jacket, snapped and stepped and shrieked to the music, this time with more than 100 talented extras moving along with him."[50]

The Queen of Pop

Jackson's success earned him the title the King of Pop. In the mid-1980s he shared his reign with the Queen of Pop, Madonna Louise Ciccone, known simply as Madonna. Born in a Detroit suburb in 1958, Madonna studied dance, singing, and drumming in her teen years. In 1983 Madonna had her first major breakthrough with the platinum album *Madonna*, filled with up-tempo songs featuring synthesizers and disco drumbeats.

Madonna cultivated a provocative sound and a look calculated to take advantage of the MTV road to stardom. In January 1984 she appeared on the popular TV show *American Bandstand*, telling the host Dick Clark, "I'm going to rule the world."[51] By the end of the year, Madonna's bold statement had come true. Her dance-rock LP *Like a Virgin* entered the *Billboard* album charts at number three in December. The album hit number one in February and by the end of 1985, *Like a Virgin* had sold 5 million copies.

Musically, *Like a Virgin* was in a style called new wave, which melded disco, rock, sixties pop, and synthesizer, or synth-based, electronic music. Produced by Nile Rodgers, one of the pioneers of 1970s disco, singles from the album such as "Angel," "Material Girl," and "Like a Virgin" were light and catchy, easy to dance to, and just plain fun.

In the videos for *Like a Virgin*, Madonna was among the first MTV stars to brazenly flaunt her sexuality. The *Like a Virgin* video shows her first in a virginal white wedding gown wandering through a fairytale castle. This is contrasted with shots of Madonna dancing suggestively on a gondola in Venice, Italy. Feminist critic Camille Paglia describes this character as "a courtesan in black, a slutty nun-turned-harlequin flapping a gold cross and posturing, bum in air, like a demonic phantom."[52]

She Is a Material Girl

In her video for the hit single "Material Girl," Madonna dresses like fifties movie star and sex symbol Marilyn Monroe. In the middle of the 1980s, a decade defined by what music critic Anthony DeCurtis calls "brutal superficiality and greed,"[53] Madonna sings that she is a material girl, more interested in wealth than in love or romance.

By modern standards, the songs on *Like a Virgin* sound innocent and cute, but Madonna generated intense controversy when millions of girls began to imitate her fashion

Madonna fans were drawn to the pop star because of both her danceable, synth-heavy songs and her provocative fashion sense.

style. After the success of the videos, every mall in America was filled with girls of all ages wearing Madonna fashions that included platinum blond hair, short lacy skirts, fingerless lace gloves, dangling earrings, bustiers, fishnet stockings, large crucifixes, strings of chains and necklaces, and dozens of bangle bracelets. Conservative social critics were aghast by what they saw as Madonna's hypersexuality shamelessly corrupting the nation's youth. Liberals blamed Madonna for portraying women as sex objects while glorifying greed.

Despite her critics, Madonna had seven top-five singles in 1985, including four number-ones. That year she also starred in her first movie, *Desperately Seeking Susan*. In the years that followed, Madonna remained at the top of the pop charts with the number-one albums *True Blue*, *Like a Prayer*, and *Erotica*. In the 1980s she sold more than 70 million records worldwide, generating $1.2 billion for Warner Bros. Records.

In 1990 Madonna continued to reign as the Queen of Pop, making headlines with her Blond Ambition World Tour. During performances of "Like a Virgin," Madonna simulated sex acts with several dancers, which prompted Christian groups to picket her shows. Even Pope John Paul II was concerned, and he urged Catholics to boycott Madonna for her sacrilegious use of Christian imagery. The controversy helped sell records, and in 1992 Madonna signed a $60 million record deal with Time/Warner, making her the highest-paid female pop star in history at that time.

Prince Generates Controversy

While Madonna capitalized on the cash-generating power of controversy, she was joined by Prince Rogers Nelson,

Parents Are Frightened

In the mid-1980s Prince was an international superstar. While he was beloved by music critics and fans alike, not everyone was thrilled by Prince's success. Tipper Gore overheard her 12-year-old daughter, Karenna, listening to "Darling Nikki" and was outraged. The song, the fifth track on *Purple Rain*, had a hard-driving funk beat and sexually explicit lyrics. Today Gore is recognized as a committed environmentalist, but at the time she was known mainly as the wife of Tennessee senator Al Gore, who went on to be elected vice president in 1992.

In 1985 Tipper Gore tuned in to MTV for several days. She was later quoted as saying, "The images frightened my children! They frightened me! I am frightened! Way frightened! The graphic sex and the violence were too much for us to handle." Gore soon formed the Parents Music Resource Center (PMRC) to protest records, videos, and concert performances believed to be violent or obscene.

The PMRC forced record companies to place warning labels on suggestive LPs. This label, which is still used today, is sometimes called the Tipper sticker. It is meant to warn parents that the music may be unsuitable for younger listeners. One of the first parental advisory stickers was applied to the Prince single "Gotta Stop (Messin' About)" from *Dirty Mind*. Since then, the sticker has been used to warn parents about sexually explicit lyrics, songs about violence and drug use, and even heavy metal songs that make reference to the occult and witchcraft.

Quoted in Kevin Egan, "Tipper Gore to be Inducted into Rock 'n Roll Hall of Fame." Word Press.com, January 22, 2009. http://operationitch.wordpress.com/2009/01/22/tipper-gore-to-be-inducted-into-rock-'n-roll-hall-of-fame.

known simply as Prince. Born in Minneapolis, Minnesota, in 1958, Prince was a musical genius in high school, and in 1978 he played every instrument on his first LP, *For You*. By the time Prince released his third album, *Dirty Mind*, in 1980, he was generating a media storm courtesy of his sexually explicit lyrics on songs like "Head" and "Sister." In concert, Prince created an androgynous, sexual image, performing in a studded purple overcoat worn over jockey shorts, knee-high boots, and leg warmers. *Dirty Mind* was certified gold and Prince's next album, appropriately titled *Controversy*, reached number-three on *Billboard*'s R&B charts.

In 1982 Prince released the double album *1999*, which quickly went triple platinum. The title song "1999" is about partying as if the world is about to end. MTV helped Prince's career when it began showing the video for another song on the *1999* album, "Little Red Corvette," which became his first top-ten hit. With a funky beat, hand claps, a synth-driven sound, and sing-along chorus, "Little Red Corvette" was in the tradition of the great American car songs pioneered by Chuck Berry and the Beach Boys.

Prince was now a major pop star. His 1984 album *Purple Rain* went on to sell more than 30 million copies worldwide, and spent twenty-four weeks at number one on *Billboard's* album chart. The album generated three chart-topping singles: "Let's Go Crazy," "Purple Rain," and "When Doves Cry." *Purple Rain* was released along with a film of the same name, a semiautobiographical account of Prince's troubled teenage home life and his rise to fame. Prince was widely recognized for his success in 1985, winning two Grammy Awards for the album *Purple Rain*. The film, which grossed more than $80 million, won an Academy Award for Best Original Song.

The Queen of Rock and Roll

During an era when young stars like Prince and Madonna were grabbing headlines, nothing surprised rock critics more than the comeback success of Tina Turner. Born Anna Mae Bullock in Nutbush, Tennessee, in 1939, Turner was 45 years old when she released the hit-filled album *Private Dancer* in 1984.

Turner first rose to fame in the 1960s singing with her husband in the Ike & Tina Turner Revue. The duo had several top-ten hits and warmed up for the Rolling Stones on their 1969 world tour. During this time, Turner says she was beaten and abused by her husband. She left him in 1976

Tina Turner, who first hit the pop scene in 1960, experienced a career revival in the 1980s with the release of Private Dancer, *which sold more than 20 million copies and produced five hit singles.*

with only thirty-eight cents in her pocket. After releasing several critically acclaimed but poor-selling albums, Turner released *Private Dancer* and achieved what rock critic Ken Tucker calls "one of the most spectacular comebacks in pop music history."[54]

The *Private Dancer* song "What's Love Got to Do with It?" hit number one and received three Grammy Awards and the video won Best Female Video at the MTV Music Awards. *Private Dancer* went on to sell more than 20 million copies and produced five top-ten singles. The videos from *Private Dancer* singles became MTV staples and Turner became renowned for her short skirts, high heels, and what *Ebony* magazine called her "famous shapely legs."[55]

In the aftermath of *Private Dancer*'s success, Turner released a best-selling autobiography, *I, Tina*, which was turned into the critically acclaimed 1993 movie *What's Love Got to Do with It*. Turner's subsequent albums went platinum. With her unique gruff voice, tinged with both anger and vulnerability, critics began calling Turner the Queen of Rock and Roll. After her initial success, she remained on the charts for decades. In 2008 her series of concerts called Tina!: 50th Anniversary Tour sold out ninety shows in North America and Europe, earning $131 million.

Rock Meets Reggae

Turner may have been crowned the Queen of Rock and Roll, but her sound was a highly polished, synthesizer-driven dance pop. Guitar-driven rock and roll in the MTV era was kept alive by several acts that featured traditional rock instruments. The English rock band the Police powered to the top of the charts as a three-piece group consisting of Sting on lead vocals and bass, Andy Summers on guitar, and Stewart Copeland playing drums.

While three-piece rock acts in the 1960s were generally heavy psychedelic bands like Cream and the Jimi Hendrix Experience, the Police played memorable rock songs that incorporated jazz and elements of rhythmic Jamaican reggae. While reggae superstars like Bob Marley were never considered pop artists, the infectious Jamaican rhythm, with a strong accent on the offbeat, was incorporated by the Police into a style called reggae rock. Although the Police were only on the scene from late 1979 to 1984, they produced a string of number-one singles that included "Roxanne," "Don't Stand So Close To Me," "Every Breath You Take," and "Every Little Thing She Does Is Magic."

Springsteen's American Family

Bruce Springsteen, whose hit "Born to Run" made him a rock star in 1975, achieved dizzying popularity in the 1980s and early 1990s. Springsteen's videos often featured him playing live in concert backed by the E Street Band. With organ, piano, saxophone, guitars, drums, and bass, Springsteen and the E Street Band provided an exciting rock-and-roll antidote to the synth sounds of the era. Springsteen also

Bruce Springsteen's 1984 hit album Born in the U.S.A., *along with his everyman persona and energetic live performances, made him one of the dominant pop artists of that decade.*

supplied something else that many rock fans sorely missed during the 1980s. He was, and remains, a politically minded performer who sings about the tough times facing blue-collar workers, farmers, and war veterans.

Springsteen's beliefs are apparent on his 1984 album *Born in the U.S.A.*, which sold more than 15 million copies. The title track describes a down-and-out Vietnam War veteran who lost his brother in the war, his faith in America, and his hope for financial security during hard economic times. Ironically, many people heard the bellowing chorus line "Born in the U.S.A." as an ode to patriotism, rather than a critique of the economic policies that Springsteen felt were enriching a few while leaving average Americans behind. In 1987 Springsteen explained his belief that when one American is suffering, everyone suffers:

> The idea of America as a family is naïve, maybe sentimental or simplistic. But it's a good idea. And if people are sick and hurting and lost, I guess it falls on everybody to address those problems in some fashion, because injustice, and the price of that injustice, falls on everyone's head . . . and steals everyone's freedom. Your wife can't walk down the street at night. People keep guns in their homes. They live with a greater sense of apprehension, anxiety and fear.[56]

Springsteen is an extremely successful rock star who retains his common touch. His fans were able to relate to him on a personal level even as he was making more money on a day-to-day basis in 1986 than Madonna, Prince, or Tina Turner. The type of people who populated Springsteen's songs—the poor, the alienated, and the hopeless—gave rock and roll a new twist in the late 1980s.

Nevermind Grunge

Guitarist, singer, and songwriter Kurt Cobain could have easily been a character in a Springsteen song. He grew up in Aberdeen, Washington, a depressed logging town 100 miles (161km) from Seattle, wracked by high unemployment, crime, drugs, and other social problems. Cobain had a poverty-stricken childhood, aggravated by his parents' di-

Singer and guitarist Kurt Cobain performs in 1993 with his band Nirvana, one of the most successful groups to come out of the Seattle grunge scene in the late 1980s and early 1990s.

vorce when he was 8. In high school, Cobain was a troubled teen whose dark moods frightened his classmates. As he told music critic Jon Savage, "They were afraid [of me]. I always felt they would vote me Most Likely to Kill Everyone at a High School Dance."[57]

Cobain found solace in music, forming the band Nirvana in 1987 with bassist Krist Novoselic. Drummer Dave Grohl joined the group in 1990. During this era there were several bands in the Seattle area that combined rock, punk, and heavy metal music into a new sound called grunge. Fueled by fuzz-tone guitars with sludgy distortion and feedback, grunge music was a rejection of the slick pop music that dominated Top 40 radio. In sharp contrast to the glittery superstars on MTV, grunge musicians like Cobain wore stringy long hair, torn jeans, tennis shoes, and dirty flannel shirts.

Despite Cobain's intense dislike of the pop music business, he became an accidental rock star in September 1991 with the release of *Nevermind*. The album contained the number-one song "Smells Like Teen Spirit." Driven by the success of the single, *Nevermind* was outselling Michael Jackson's highly publicized *Dangerous* LP in early 1992.

"Smells Like Teen Spirit" combines distorted, heavy metal power chords and thunderous drumming with dreamy, melodic verses and an infectious, scream-along chorus. The video for the song was shot to purposely look amateurish and homemade. It is based on a concept of a high school pep rally that ends in a riot as students destroy the band's gear. MTV played the video so relentlessly that it entered the *Guinness World Records* book in 2000 as the Most Played Video.

Nirvana's next album *In Utero* entered the charts at number one and quickly sold 4 million copies. By this time, Cobain, deeply depressed over his personal life and sudden fame, had become addicted to heroin. According to rock journalist Greil Marcus, Cobain was gripped by "the suspicion that if what you do is accepted by a mass audience, then your work must be either devoid of content or a sell-out, and you yourself the enemy you set out to destroy."[58] He died from a self-inflicted gunshot wound to the head on April 5, 1994, at the age of twenty-seven.

Although they did not wish it, Nirvana helped grunge music achieve respectability. In 1992 *Time* magazine noted, "Smells Like Teen Spirit" had become "an anthem for apathetic kids,"[59] while the rough-looking video helped change the look of music videos.

Headbangers Have a Ball

The power chords of grunge helped renew widespread interest in heavy metal music, which had peaked in popularity in the 1980s. The MTV show *Headbangers Ball*, which featured videos by bands like Judas Priest, Metallica, Mötley Crüe, Megadeath, Anthrax, and Slayer, shined a spotlight on heavy metal players for a new generation.

By 1987 *Headbangers Ball* was the most watched show on MTV, which pushed heavy metal music up the charts. In the early 1990s, about half of all albums on *Billboard*'s top twenty were by heavy metal bands. While the music was as fast, loud, and belligerent as any rock and roll, the stars of *Headbangers Ball* had big hair, outrageous clothes, and exuded controversy. In other words, they were perfect fodder for MTV. The music was rowdier than Madonna and angrier than Prince and made millions of dollars for the entertainment corporations that provided heavy metal pop music for apathetic American teens.

CHAPTER 6

Hip Hop and Teen Pop

In 1999 the traditional record industry business model fell apart when peer-to-peer (P2P) file sharing was introduced on the Internet. The traditional business model, which began around 1904, had been a great success for the music industry. Music was tightly controlled and released only on records, cassette tapes, or compact discs (CDs) that could be purchased by fans. The advent of P2P, however, allowed a computer user, or peer, to search for and download specific song files stored on the computers of anonymous peers anywhere in the world. P2P file sharing allowed music lovers to obtain music for free.

The cost of P2P file sharing to the music industry is compiled by the trade group the Recording Industry Association of America (RIAA). In 2009 the RIAA determined that in the decade after P2P file sharing emerged in 1999, music sales in the United States dropped 47 percent, from $14.6 billion to $7.7 billion. From 2004 through 2009 alone, approximately 30 billion songs were illegally downloaded on file-sharing networks.

These changes in the music business had a negative impact on music in general. As revenues fell, record companies were less willing to spend the money necessary to develop new talent. In earlier eras record companies would allow bands to record several albums that might not have topped the charts but that attracted growing legions of fans. For example, Pink Floyd made its first album in 1967 but did not become a supergroup until 1973. In the 2000s, if a record company did not think a new band could produce

The Failings of the Music Industry

The music industry has been blaming illegal downloads for its problems since the late 1990s. Singer-songwriter Ramin Streets lists other commonly accepted reasons for the financial failings of the music business:

> At some point along the way (late 70s) label executives became . . . more interested in keeping their jobs and playing it safe vs. finding authentic and original talent to nurture and promote over the long haul. We used to have an industry focused on finding the next new and amazing thing. . . . Gone are the days of breaking out of the mold. For the last few decades it's been about formula. . . . Signed artists no longer have the staying power, personality or song writing abilities of their predecessors. . . . As such for the most part we don't remember many artists or "hit" songs from the last 20 years. . . . [We] now have artists calling themselves songwriters with little knowledge of music theory, composition or song structure or appreciation for styles that came before (to our detriment). . . .
>
> [Another problem is] the music industry has abused fans in the U.S. with both unnecessarily high CD prices and obscenely high concert ticket prices. CDs cost pennies to manufacture yet cost the consumer upwards of $20 for a product that in most cases has delivered 1–2 decent tracks at best with the remainder serving only as filler.

Ramin Streets. "Top 10 Reasons Why the Music Industry is Failing." HubPages. http://hubpages.com/hub/Top-10-Reasons-Why-the-Music-Industry-is-Failing.

a platinum-selling record right away, it would not offer a recording contract. As a result, in 2010 the number of new musical acts signed by record companies was the lowest in history.

Some critics argue that the lack of fresh, innovative talent can be traced to the drop of record sales and, thus, the tighter grip that record companies had on signing new acts. The major worldwide financial recession, which began in 2008, has also been blamed. Because of the music industry's woes, most twenty-first-century pop stars no longer expect to earn as much from record sales as they did in the past. In order to make up for the financial shortfall, some artists sell their songs for use in commercials, a practice largely frowned upon by earlier generations of rock stars. In addition, many pop stars diversify and sell a wide range of products not related to music, such as perfumes, colognes, clothing, sports drinks, and video games.

Inner-city Hip Hop

In the twenty-first century, the most successful pop stars are hip-hop artists. When the music first appeared in New York City in 1977, mindless disco dance music and arena rock bands like Fleetwood Mac topped the charts. It seemed highly unlikely that hip hop would someday become the dominant form of pop music, with its themes centered on gang violence and social problems set to the sound of rapid-fire spoken poetry and scratched vinyl records. Hip-hop promoter and journalist Dan Charnas explains: "[Hip hop was produced by] a marginal subculture confined to the two most notorious ghettos in the United States, Harlem and the South Bronx."[60]

Hip-hop innovators chanted rhythmic poetry called rap. Performers, called rappers, used their mouths to beat box, a technique that emulates drum machines, record-scratching on turntables, and other percussive effects. In the 1980s, new digital devices, such as the E-mu Emulator, allowed rappers to sample short segments of sounds from other recordings and paste them together to form a new sound. The technique of sampling became the centerpiece of hip-hop

music production. Hip-hop journalist Nelson George explains how the quirky trio De La Soul sampled pop hits for their 1988 album *3 Feet High and Rising*:

> [The song] 'Eye Know' features Steely Dan's 'Peg' rubbing up against Otis Redding's 'Dock of the Bay,' and on [the song] 'Say No Go,' Sly Stone fragments meet the Hall and Oates hook from 'I Can't Go for That.' Over these crafty [sampled] tracks, rappers Trugoy and Posdnuos intone their lyrics with a witty conversational ease.[61]

Sampling has generated as much controversy as some of the hard-core lyrics of hip hop. Many lawsuits were filed by artists whose music was used without permission. In one notable example, soul singer Rick James sued rapper M.C. Hammer for using his 1981 hit "Super Freak." Hammer sampled the song in his 1990 chart-topping "U Can't Touch This." The lawsuit was settled when Hammer agreed to credit James as a co-writer. This brought James millions of dollars in songwriting royalties.

De La Soul, with members (from left) Vincent Mason, David Jude Jolicoeur, and Kevin Mercer, sampled a range of pop songs on their 1988 album 3 Feet High and Rising.

Hip hop might have remained confined to black audiences in inner-city neighborhoods. However, the music was introduced to white teenagers thanks to the relentless promotional efforts by two producers, Russell Simmons and Rick Rubin. In the mid-1980s the men founded Def Jam Records and made mainstream stars of Run-D.M.C., LL Cool J, and one of the first white rap groups, the Beastie Boys. These acts widened hip hop's appeal beyond urban areas and popularized the sound in America's white suburbs. Kyle Stewart, a white hip-hop fan, explains his attraction to hip-hop music: "Like punk, hip hop was counterculture. It gave youth a voice to tell the truth and exposed the ills of society, especially racism and our hypocritical government. Also, the beats were infectious."[62] For fans like Stewart, hip hop was an updated version of Little Richard's wild beat in the 1950s or Bob Dylan's social commentary of the 1960s.

Gangsta Rap

Hip hop remained controversial throughout the 1980s despite support from white fans and platinum-selling albums such as *Run-D.M.C.*, which features aggressive rhymes about ghetto life. When Run-D.M.C. played a concert in Long Beach, California, in 1985, about three hundred black and Hispanic gang members swarmed through the crowd attacking everyone around them. Even though this was an isolated event, parents and politicians became afraid of hip hop. Harvard psychiatrist Alvin Poussaint called hip hop fans "inner-city street kids, some of whom are gang members immersed in antisocial behavior."[63] The rise of rapper Tupac "2Pac" Shakur in the early 1990s confirmed these fears for many.

2Pac was born in Harlem, New York, in 1971 and grew up in a violent household. Various members of his family were convicted of crimes ranging from bank robbery to the murder of a police officer. As a young child, 2Pac was artistic and creative. He first acted in theatrical productions when he was twelve years old, and later studied acting, poetry, jazz, and ballet. 2Pac also entered rap competitions as a teenager, which helped him develop the techniques of a master gangsta rapper. Gangsta rap is a genre of hip-hop that focuses on gangs, violence, sex, crack cocaine, marijuana, alcohol, materialism, fighting the police, and the brutality of inner-city life. Rapping about such topics made 2Pac and other gangsta rappers like Ice T and Notorious B.I.G. extremely popular among both black fans and white suburban teens.

White fans helped make 2Pac one of the biggest names in hip-hop practically overnight. His two-volume CD *All Eyez On Me* sold 5 million copies within two months of its April 1996 release and produced two number-one singles, "How Do U Want It?" and "California Love." Jeremy Miller, a white 2Pac fan, explained his love of the album: "In terms of the beats, the way the words are put over the music, it's just powerful music to me and I think the white kids that are into it now really feel the power in the music."[64]

Controversy usually drives music sales, and dozens of press reports about 2Pac's "gangsta" lifestyle doubtlessly helped sell his CDs. 2Pac was arrested for committing sexual assault in 1993 and found guilty in November 1994. Several days before his conviction, he was shot five times during a robbery in his New York studio. After serving a prison sentence for the assault charge, 2Pac was shot and killed in Las Vegas, Nevada, on September 6, 1996. He was twenty-five years old. The murder was never solved. 2Pac albums continued to sell long after his death and, as of 2011, more than 75 million albums were sold worldwide, making him one of the most successful music acts of all time.

By the end of the 1990s, gangsta rap was the most lucrative form of hip hop and one of the most successful styles of pop music. Many hip hoppers took advantage of this situation. West Coast rapper Snoop Dogg became an international celebrity after releasing platinum-selling albums that celebrated hard partying and an opulent lifestyle. Like many pop stars before him, Snoop Dogg took up acting, appearing in movies and TV shows and lending his voice to animated films. Another former gangsta, Ice-T became famous for his controversial "Cop Killer" single in 1992. Ironically, in 2000, Ice-T gave up his hip-hop career to portray a police detective on the TV drama *Law & Order: Special Victims Unit*.

Tycoon Diddy

Among all the pioneers of gangsta rap, no one has become a more successful tycoon than Sean John Combs, known by the stage names Puff Daddy, P. Diddy, and Diddy. Combs was born in 1969, grew up in the suburb of Mount Vernon, New York, and dropped out of college in 1993 to found Bad Boy Records with the rapper Notorious B.I.G. After promoting various hip-hop artists and writing successful songs

Rapper Sean "Diddy" Combs performs at the MTV Europe Music Awards in 1999. Combs has built a business empire as a promoter, performer, producer, fashion designer, and restaurateur.

for female gangsta rapper Lil' Kim and others, Combs recorded his first solo album, *No Way Out*, in 1997. The first single from the album, "Can't Nobody Hold Me Down," spent six weeks at number-one on the *Billboard* Hot 100. The album produced another number-one single, "I'll Be Missing You," and two number-two singles, "Been Around the World" and "It's All about the Benjamins." These songs made extensive use of sampling, and the album *No Way Out* included bits and pieces of songs including "Let's Dance" by David Bowie, "You Haven't Done Nothin'" by Stevie Wonder, and "Every Breath You Take" by the Police.

While critics considered Combs a weak rapper, he understood there was a market for less controversial gangsta rap. Combs became a pop star by toning down the most objectionable aspects of the genre. In his videos and television appearances, Combs projects an image of success and cool stylishness rather than the ghetto hardness of 2Pac. Instead of rapping about discrimination, drug dealing, and violence, he rapped about an extravagant lifestyle filled with diamonds, cars, and gorgeous women. This helped drive Diddy's follow-up albums, such as 2002's *We Invented the Remix* and 2006's *Press Play*, to the top of the charts.

Combs, always a shrewd businessman and self-promoter, used his fame to create a marketing empire unlike any other pop star. In 1998 he started a clothing line called Sean John and his fashion designs earned him consecutive nominations for Menswear Designer of the Year between 2000 and 2005. Sean John also produces a popular cologne. In addition, Combs owns an upscale restaurant chain called Justin's. In 2011 he was worth an estimated $475 million, making him the wealthiest figure in hip hop.

Gangsta Returns to Its Roots

Diddy's raps helped hip hop become more acceptable to mainstream audiences, but it also created something of a backlash. Those who felt hip hop was never meant to be pop music flocked to artists like 50 Cent (Curtis James Jackson III) and Eminem (Marshall Mathers). These rappers achieved multiplatinum success with violent words and thuggish deeds that shocked and offended many.

50 Cent grew up in a New York ghetto with a drug-dealing mother. As a teenager, he learned to box, became a crack dealer, and went to prison. His hip hop career was on the rise in 2000 when he was shot nine times in retaliation for a robbery. 50 Cent barely survived, but he kept rapping. In 2002 one of his tapes was given to Eminem, who signed him to a $1 million record deal. The result was the much anticipated autobiographical *Get Rich or Die Tryin'*, which mixed catchy sing-along hooks, roughneck raps, and the story of 50 Cent's rise from poverty to fame. The album, which debuted at number-one, sold 15 million copies.

After attaining crossover pop success, 50 Cent engaged in a marketing frenzy. He founded G-Unit Clothing Company, signed a long-term deal with Reebok, produced a video game called *50 Cent: Bulletproof,* set up a film company, acted in several movies, and started a reality show on MTV. 50 Cent also sponsored a vitamin water and a body spray. In 2011 his estimated net worth was more than $150 million.

Teen Pop and Boy Bands

Throughout the 1990s and early 2000s, record companies marketed hip-hop and gangsta rap to adult music fans, typically those seventeen to twenty-five years old, but they also took advantage of the multibillion-dollar teen pop industry aimed at younger fans. Beginning in the mid-1990s, wholesome teen pop "boy bands" like the Backstreet Boys, *NSYNC, and 98 Degrees produced albums aimed at the ten- to sixteen-year-old demographic.

Teen pop acts blended dance music, R&B ballads, and pop rock. The songs are usually composed by professional songwriters, performed by older teens, and aimed squarely at younger music fans. While the lyrics or dance moves in the videos might be slightly provocative, most teen pop is clean, catchy, and very commercial.

One of the most successful teen pop bands, the Backstreet Boys, was formed in 1993 in Orlando, Florida, by five sing-

crs: Nick Carter, Howie Dorough, Brian Littrell, A.J. McLean, and Kevin Richardson. The group's first album, 1996's *Backstreet Boys*, was a hit in Europe, while their second album, *Backstreet's Back*, drove the group to the top of the pop charts in 1997. With their seamless vocal harmonies and synchronized dance moves, the Backstreet Boys were reminiscent of 1960s Motown groups like the Four Tops and the Temptations.

While rooted in the soul tradition, the Backstreet Boys introduced a modern sound called new jack swing to their musical mix. The style mixes hip-hop drum-machine beats, synthesizers, and bass-heavy sound samples into R&B ballads. The new jack swing on Backstreet Boys albums like *Millennium* and *Black & Blue* helped the group appeal to a large audience—blacks, whites, preteens, teens, and even adults. Radio music director Jay Michaels explains, "[The Backstreet Boys] have an image of clean-cut, upbeat pop music that kids like. But they also appeal to adults . . . the lyrics really hit home with women. Appealing to kids and adults is ideal for top 40."[65] The Backstreet Boys' crossover appeal helped them sell more than 130 million records worldwide, making them the best-selling boy band in history.

The Backstreet Boys, performing in 2005, were one of several "boy bands" put together in the late 1990s and early 2000s by producers looking to capture the teen pop market.

*NSYNC's Dirty Pop

The boy band *NSYNC was the main competition for the Backstreet Boys in the late nineties. Made up of members JC Chasez, Justin Timberlake, Chris Kirkpatrick, Joey Fatone, and Lance Bass, *NSYNC combined danceable beats, R&B harmonies, and appealing male singers into a formula for superstar success. The group's 2000 CD *No Strings Attached* is a little edgier than most teen pop offerings. The album's style, labeled dirty pop by the band, features gritty street beats, Timberlake's beat boxing, and occasionally snarling vocals. The album sold more than 2.4 million copies its first week, setting a one-week sales record.

*NSYNC broke up in 2002 and Timberlake went on to become one of the most successful singers in pop history. His first two solo albums, 2002's *Justified* and 2006's *FutureSex/LoveSounds*, each sold more than 7 million copies. Like other twenty-first-century pop stars, Timberlake also created a business empire away from the music industry. He is financially involved in three restaurants, has his own brand of tequila called 901, and owns the William Rast clothing line.

From Mouseketeers to Pop Stars

Timberlake began his career in 1995 on the Disney Channel television show *The All-New Mickey Mouse Club*, which featured comedy skits and songs. Amazingly, the show featured two other cast members that year who went on to become pop superstars: Britney Spears and Christina Aguilera.

Spears became a major pop sensation at the age of seventeen, when the single ". . . Baby One More Time" debuted in late 1998. The song, which combines rap-influenced dance pop and smooth, light vocals, sounds like typical teen pop of the era for a good reason. The song was composed by Swedish music producer Max Martin, who also wrote chart-topping teen pop hits for the Backstreet Boys, *NSYNC, Katy Perry, and Pink.

". . . Baby One More Time" shot to number one as the video generated controversy. Spears dances down a high school hallway dressed in a Catholic school uniform with

Beyoncé's Destiny

Beyoncé Knowles is one of most successful music artists of all time, selling more than 75 million records and earning sixteen Grammy Awards. Born in Houston, Texas, in 1981, Beyoncé was destined for stardom. She began singing, dancing, and performing in talent shows at the age of 7. By high school she had formed the group Destiny's Child, which topped the charts in 1999 with the album *The Writing's on the Wall*. It soon became clear to critics and the public that Beyoncé was the breakout star of Destiny's Child thanks to her unique singing style that merged hip-hop sensibilities with soulful R&B.

When Beyoncé released her first solo album, *Dangerously in Love*, in June 2003, it entered the charts at number one. The infectious lead single, "Crazy in Love," stayed at number one for two months. Beyoncé's second album, *B'Day*, was released on her 25th birthday in 2006 and produced a number of hit singles. Beyoncé's third studio album, *I Am . . . Sasha Fierce*, debuted at number one upon its release in 2008. Beyoncé has also had a successful movie career, appearing in *The Pink Panther*, *Dreamgirls*, and *Cadillac Records*. In addition, Beyoncé has her own clothing line and fragrance, and she founded the Survivor Charity, a community outreach organization.

the shirt tied up in a revealing manner. Because Spears was still in high school herself, some were offended by her oversexed image. The album *. . . Baby One More Time* quickly sold 10 million copies and eventually went on to sell 26 million. In 2011 it was listed by *Guinness World Records* as the best-selling album by a teenage solo artist. Spears's follow-up album, *Oops! . . . I Did It Again*, sold about 20 million copies.

Despite the racy image she projected in videos and concerts, Spears claimed to be a religious, wholesome teen who believed in abstinence until marriage and other conservative values. In 2000 when Spears revealed she had been dating *NSYNC member Justin Timberlake for several years, she became the central focus of the tabloid media. The couple broke up in 2002 and Spears soon became better known for her various romances, marriages, divorces, and drug-addled behavior than her music—even as her albums continued to achieve multiplatinum status. Fans could not get enough of Spears, and in 2009 her world concert tour, The Circus Starring Britney Spears, was the top-grossing act of the year, bringing in more than $131 million.

Rolling Stone called Spears's 2011 album, *Femme Fatale*, her best. The album is filled with fast-tempo synth pop and drum-machine-driven electric dance hooks aimed at capturing an international audience. Commenting on her importance in the modern music scene, Caryn Ganz of *Rolling Stone* writes, "Along with the Backstreet Boys and 'N Sync, [Spears] spearheaded the rise of post-millennial teen pop. . . . [And] cultivated a mixture of innocence and experience that generated lots of cash."[66]

Guitar-Wielding Bad Girl

During the 2000s, Spears was among the largest group of talented female singers in pop music history. Beyoncé, Christina Aguilera, Rihanna, Pink, Katy Perry, and Kelly Clarkson, along with older artists like Mariah Carey and Madonna, sold millions of albums filled with dance pop, R&B, soul, and pop hits. The decade was also ripe for young female rockers, like Canadian Avril Lavigne, who wanted to be recognized for their singing, songwriting, and guitar playing rather than their sex appeal.

Like Spears, Lavigne was only seventeen when she became famous. Unlike the controversial Spears, Lavigne seemed more comfortable in jeans and tank tops, the outfit she wore in the video of her debut single "Complicated" in 2002. The song was released on the album *Let Go*, which quickly sold 6 million copies. Lavigne's appeal as a punky, guitar-wielding, skateboarding bad girl endeared her to millions worldwide when she appeared in the videos for "Complicated" and "Sk8r Boi." With *Let Go*, Lavigne be-

Avril Lavigne's punky bad-girl image made her stand out from other female performers when she came on the pop scene in 2002 at age seventeen, but her music evolved to reflect a more serious, mature artist.

came the youngest female musician to ever have a number-one album in the United Kingdom. Her concert tour in support of the album took her to Australia, Asia, North America, and Europe, and *Let Go* was nominated for eight Grammys in 2003.

Despite her pop success, Lavigne was determined to be taken seriously as a soulful singer, musician, and songwriter. Her second album, 2004's *Under My Skin*, dealt with troubling issues such as depression and the heartbreaking death of her grandfather. The album went platinum within a month. With the release of her fourth album, *Goodbye Lullaby*, in 2011, Lavigne continued to explore raw emotions and personal pain with mellow ballads like "Goodbye," "Everybody Hurts," and "Wish You Were Here."

Like other teen idols, Lavigne launched her own clothing line, called Abbey Dawn, and released a fragrance, *Black Star*. However, she is also known for her charitable work. Lavigne promotes various environmental and humanitarian organizations and in 2010 she launched The Avril Lavigne Foundation to help young people with serious illnesses and disabilities.

Teen sensation Justin Bieber first rose to fame by posting music videos of his performances on YouTube.

Bieber's World

Lavigne was Canada's best-known pop export until 2009, when her fame was eclipsed by a fifteen-year-old singer from London, Ontario. Justin Bieber was only twelve when he began posting performance videos on YouTube. A video of an R&B song of his was accidentally discovered by an American talent scout named Scott "Scooter" Braun, who was searching for a different artist at the time. Braun was impressed enough to fly Bieber to Atlanta, Georgia, for an audition. A week later, the young singer was signed to a recording contract.

When Bieber's first single "One Time" was released in May 2009, he became the biggest teenage pop star since Michael Jackson. By January 2010, the video of "One Time," posted to YouTube, had been viewed more than

Rihanna

In 2005, 17-year-old singer Rihanna (Robyn Rihanna Fenty) combined the island sound of reggae with dance pop and R&B on her debut single "Pon de Replay," and the Barbados-born Rihanna quickly became an international singing sensation.

Rihanna had star qualities even as a young girl, often winning talent shows and beauty contests. She was discovered in 2005 by Evan Rogers, who was vacationing in Barbados with his wife. Rogers was an extremely successful pop producer whose roster included superstars *NSYNC, Christina Aguilera, and Jessica Simpson. Rogers offered Rihanna a chance to record, but her first two albums, *Music of the Sun* and *A Girl Like Me*, were not well-received by critics, who compared her unfavorably to Beyoncé. Music reviewers changed their minds with Rihanna's third album, 2007's *Good Girl Gone Bad*, which features up-tempo, soulful dance tracks with an island flavor. Since then, Rihanna has collaborated on hits with rapper Eminem, released two more albums (*Rated R* and *Loud*), written a book, and signed several lucrative endorsement deals for various products. By 2011, Rihanna had sold 15 million albums and 45 million singles, making her one of best-selling artists of all time.

100 million times. *One Time* is the fifth most-viewed video in YouTube history, a fitting tribute for the first YouTube pop star. It is notable that despite Bieber's role as a teen idol, the song never reached number one on the *Billboard* charts. It has been downloaded illegally countless times from file-sharing sites.

Bieber's seven-song extended-play (EP) album *My World*, which contains "One Time," went platinum during its first week of release. While reviewers describe his songs with terms like puppy-love ballads, bubbly synths, and dinky dance pop, Bieber's fanatical female fans have made him an inescapable pop sensation. His follow-up album, 2010's *My World 2.0*, debuted at number-one on the album charts. This made Bieber the youngest solo singer to accomplish this feat since a young Stevie Wonder released the album *Recorded Live: The 12 Year Old Genius* in 1963.

In 2010 Bieber experienced full media saturation. He

appeared on TV shows like *Saturday Night Live*, *The Daily Show*, and *CSI: Crime Scene Investigation*. He was on the cover of *Rolling Stone* and was featured in hundreds of magazine and newspaper articles. *My World 2.0* was nominated for Canadian Juno Awards, MTV Video Awards, Grammy Awards, Teen Choice Awards, Nickelodeon Kid's Choice Awards, and others. His 3-D concert film, *Justin Bieber: Never Say Never*, which features scenes from his 2010 concert tour My World Tour, grossed $29 million the first weekend. This figure put Bieber's movie ahead of those by other pop sensations like the Jonas Brothers' *The 3D Concert Experience* and *Michael Jackson's This Is It*. Bieber's rabid fans are called Beliebers and their fanatical devotion has left little doubt that music fans remain hungry for clean-cut teen pop idols.

Lady Gaga Finds Fame

In October 2010 YouTube recorded more than 967 million views of Bieber's videos. This would have given him a Guinness world record if not for Lady Gaga, who set a record for more than 1 billion views of her material on the video-sharing website. This is only one of the records Gaga set that year. In August 2010 she overtook Britney Spears as the most followed person on Twitter and became the first star to have more than 20 million Facebook fans. Although Lady Gaga was virtually unknown until August 2008, her appropriately titled debut album *The Fame* went straight to the top of the charts and made her an international celebrity.

Lady Gaga, born Stefani Joanne Angelina Germanotta in March 1986, is a twenty-first-century pop sensation, but her music is rooted firmly in the eighties. *The Fame* singles such as "Just Dance" and "Poker Face" incorporate 1980s-style electronic pop, dance music, and synthesizers. Lady Gaga's outrageous fashions, singing style, and dance moves have

Lady Gaga's music, boosted by her outrageous style and savvy use of social media, dominated the pop charts in 2010 and 2011.

also been compared to the queen of eighties pop, Madonna. Lady Gaga made no effort to hide her Madonna references in the 2010 video *Alejandro*. She imitates the hairstyle, scenes, and clothing from Madonna's late-eighties videos *Vogue* and *Like a Prayer*.

Perhaps in an era when samples from old songs are heard every day on new music, it is not surprising when one artist closely mimics the look of another. Despite her similarities to Madonna, Lady Gaga is obviously an original, with as many fanatical fans as Justin Bieber. Her second album, *Fame Monster*, garnered six Grammy nominations and won for Best Pop Vocal Album. She is the first artist to produce three singles that sold more than 4 million copies each. Lady Gaga has used her fame for humanitarian causes, supporting HIV/AIDS education and donating large sums to disaster relief after tragic earthquakes in Haiti and Japan.

A Musical Conversation

Hip hop and teen pop so dominated the music scene in the 2000s that the popularity of rock bands diminished. While rock groups like Blink-182, the Kings of Leon, Arcade Fire, and Vampire Weekend continued to produce platinum albums, their presence in the pop world was largely eclipsed by Bieber, Lady Gaga, 50 Cent, and others. Punk rockers Green Day were among the most successful rockers during an era when rappers and teen idols were topping the charts.

While tastes and styles change, pop music continues to shape the American culture by bringing stories alive in melody and lyric. The entire history of the style can be explored today as millions of songs from every era are available as digital downloads. From "Alexander's Ragtime Band" to "Purple Haze" to "Just Dance," thousands of pop stars got rich. Some died trying. But all have added to the musical conversation America has been having with itself for more than a hundred years.

Introduction:
Popular Music

1. Larry Starr and Christopher Waterman. *American Popular Music from Minstrelsy to MTV*. New York: Oxford University Press, 2003, p. 5.
2. Starr and Waterman. *American Popular Music*, p. 461.

Chapter 1: Musical Tales of American Life

3. Kevin Phinney. *Souled America: How Black Music Transformed White Culture*. New York: Billboard Books, 2005, p. 77.
4. Langston Hughes and Milton Meltzer. *Black Magic*. Englewood Cliffs, NJ: Prentice-Hall, 1967, p. 80.
5. Quoted in Bill C. Malone and David Stricklin. *Southern Music/American Music*. Lexington: University Press of Kentucky, 2003, p. 63.
6. Quoted in James L. Dickerson. *Mojo Triangle*. New York: Schirmer Trade Books, 2005, pp. 56–57.

Chapter 2: Rockin' Around the Clock

7. Arnold Shaw. *The Rockin' 50s*. New York: Da Capo Press, 1987, p. 17.
8. Quoted in Nathan Rabin. "Week 15: Jimmie Rodgers' White Man Blues." A.V. Club, July 7, 2009. www.avclub.com/articles/week -15-jimmie-rodgers-white-man -blues,30039.
9. Donald Clarke. *The Rise and Fall of Popular Music*. New York: St. Martin's Press, 1995, p. 365.
10. Quoted in Ed Ward, Geoffrey Stokes, and Ken Tucker. *Rock of Ages: The Rolling Stone History of Rock*. New York: Rolling Stone Press, 1986, p. 69.
11. Ward, Stokes, and Tucker. *Rock of Ages*, p. 70.
12. Fred Bronson. *The Billboard Book of Number One Hits*. New York: Billboard Books, 1997, p. xxiii.
13. Quoted in Phinney. *Souled America*, p. 14.
14. Dickerson. *Mojo Triangle*, p. 131.
15. Quoted in David Brackett, ed. *The Pop, Rock, and Soul Reader*. New York: Oxford University Press, 2005, p. 94.
16. Time. "Music: Teeners' Hero," www.time.com/time/magazine/ article/0,9171,808428,00.html, 2011.
17. Quoted in Brackett. *The Pop, Rock,*

and Soul Reader, p. 99.

18. Clarke. *The Rise and Fall of Popular Music*, p. 377.

19. Quoted in Mark Jacobson. "Chuck Berry, the Father of Rock Turns 75." *Rolling Stone*, December 6, 2001, p. 80.

20. Quoted in Holly George-Warren, ed. *Rolling Stone: The Decades of Rock & Roll*. San Francisco: Chronicle Books, 2001, p. 17.

21. Quoted in June Bundy. *Billboard*, December 15, 1958, p. 8.

Chapter 3: The Sixties Sound Explosion

22. Quoted in Robert Shelton. *No Direction Home: The Life and Music of Bob Dylan*. New York: Da Capo Press, 2003, p. 3.

23. Quoted in Charles White. *The Life and Times of Little Richard: The Authorised Biography*. London: Omnibus Press, 2003, p. 228.

24. The Beatles. *The Beatles Anthology*. San Francisco: Chronicle Books, 2000, p. 11.

25. Quoted in Anthony DeCurtis, James Henke, and Holly George-Warren, eds. *The Rolling Stone Illustrated History of Rock & Roll*. New York: Random House, 1992, p. 281.

26. Quoted in Rolling Stone. "Smokey Robinson." *Rolling Stone*, 2011. www.rollingstone.com/music/artists/smokey-robinson/biography.

27. Quoted in Brackett. *The Pop, Rock,*

and Soul Reader, p. 146.

28. Quoted in Brackett. *The Pop, Rock, and Soul Reader*, p. 146.

29. Quoted in Chris Smith. *101 Albums That Changed Popular Music*. New York: Oxford University Press, 2009, p. 46.

30. Starr and Waterman. *American Popular Music*, pp. 293–294.

31. Quoted in David Szatnary. *A Time to Rock: A Social History of Rock and Roll*. Boulder, CO: Westview, 1996, p. 107.

32. Lucy O'Brien. *She Bop*. New York: Penguin Books, 1995, p. 100.

33. Quoted in Smith. *101 Albums That Changed Popular Music*, p. 41.

Chapter 4: Big Sounds, Big Business

34. Quoted in Jeremy Harding. "The Dream is Over: Lennon in Search of Himself." Guardian UK, December 21, 2000. www.guardian.co.uk/music/2000/dec/21/thebeatles.johnlennon.

35. Marc Elliot. *Rockonomics*. New York: Franklin Watts, 1989, p. 152.

36. Starr and Waterman. *American Popular Music*, p. 314.

37. Quoted in Starr and Waterman. *American Popular Music*, p. 323.

38. Timothy White. *Rock Lives*. New York: Henry Holt, 1990, p. 288.

39. Starr and Waterman. *American Popular Music*, pp. 329–330.

40. Quoted in White. *Rock Lives*, p. 288.

41. Smith. *101 Albums That Changed*

Popular Music, p. 103.

42. Scott Schinder and Andy Schwartz. *Icons of Rock*, vol. 2. Westport, CT: Greenwood Press, 2008, p. 447.

43. Quoted in George-Warren. *Rolling Stone*, p. 148.

44. Quoted in George-Warren. *Rolling Stone*, p. 148.

45. Quoted in Tony Sclafani. "When 'Disco Sucks!' echoed around the world." MSNBC.com, July 10, 2009. http://today.msnbc.msn.com /id/31832616/ns/today-entertain ment.

Chapter 5: Video Stars and Rock Rebels

46. Quoted in Gary Burns. "Music Television." The Museum of Broadcast Communications, 2011. www.museum.tv/eotvsection .php?entrycode=musictelevis.

47. Quoted in Michael Shore. *The Rolling Stone Book of Rock Video*. New York: Quill, 1984, p. 15.

48. Robert Christgau. "Rock-n-Roller Coaster: The Music Biz on a Joyride." *Village Voice*, February 7, 1984, p. 37.

49. Tom McGrath. *MTV: The Making of a Revolution*. Philadelphia: Running Press, 1996, pp. 85–86.

50. McGrath. *MTV*, p. 101.

51. Quoted in Lucy O'Brien. *Madonna: Like an Icon*. New York: Harper-Entertainment, 2007, p. 71.

52. Quoted in Allen Metz and Carol Benson, eds. *The Madonna Companion: Two Decades of Commen-*

tary. New York: Schirmer Books, 1999, pp. 163–164.

53. Quoted in George-Warren. *Rolling Stone*, p. 173.

54. Ward, Stokes, and Tucker. *Rock of Ages*, p. 606.

55. Lynn Norment. "The Foreign Affairs of Tina Turner." *Ebony*, November 1989, p. 168.

56. Quoted in George-Warren. *Rolling Stone*, p. 185.

57. Quoted in George-Warren. *Rolling Stone*, p. 245.

58. Quoted in George-Warren. *Rolling Stone*, p. 246.

59. Time. "Winners of 1991." www .time.com/time/magazine/article /0,9171,974625,00.html, January 6, 1992.

Chapter 6: Hip Hop and Teen Pop

60. Dan Charnas. *The Big Payback: The History of the Business of Hip Hop*. New York: New American Library, 2010, p. ix.

61. Nelson George. *Hip Hop America*. New York: Penguin Books, 1998, p. 84.

62. Quoted in Bakari Kitwana. *Why White Kids Love Hip Hop: Wankstas, Wannabes, and the New Reality of Race in America*. New York: Basic Civitas Books, 2005, p. 27.

63. Quoted in *Time*. "Bad Rap." September 1, 1986, p. 20.

64. Quoted in Kitwana. *Why White Kids Love Hip Hop*, p. 30.

65. Quoted in Chuck Taylor. "Air

Waves." *Billboard*, May 23, 1998, p. 84.

66. Caryn Ganz, "Britney Spears." *Rolling Stone*, www.rollingstone.com /music/artists/britney-spears /biography, 2011.

Louis Armstrong

The Best of the Hot 5 & Hot 7 Recordings, 2002

On this album Armstrong is in his prime, playing with some of the best jazz musicians in history.

Backstreet Boys

Backstreet's Back, 1997

Beach Boys

Sounds of Summer—The Very Best of the Beach Boys, 2003

This album includes hits that inspired millions of Americans to move to California in the 1960s.

The Beatles

Sgt. Pepper's Lonely Hearts Club Band, 1967

Critics agree this is one of the most important albums in history, and according to *Rolling Stone* it is the greatest album ever made. The look and sound of *Sgt. Pepper* forever changed pop music and continues to influence musicians more than forty years after it was recorded.

1, 2000

Issued on the 30th anniversary of the band's breakup, this album, which has sold more than 31 million copies, contains every number-one Beatles song recorded between 1962 and 1970—an amazing 27 songs.

Chuck Berry

The Chess Box, 1988

This album features Chuck Berry's hits in their original form, including "Johnny B. Goode," "Maybelline," "Rock and Roll Music," and more, as they sounded in the 1950s, when Berry changed the sound of rock and roll forever.

Justin Bieber

My World, 2009

My World 2.0, 2010

Big Brother & The Holding Company

Cheap Thrills, 1999

This album, recorded live at the Fillmore in San Francisco, features Janis Joplin at her peak. Backed by one of the hottest psychedelic blues bands in Haight-Ashbury, Joplin rasps her way through George Gershwin's 1935 classic "Summertime," moans and shrieks "Piece of My Heart," and takes "Ball and Chain" to a level of intensity most white singers of the era could not even imagine.

David Bowie

Ziggy Stardust and the Spiders from Mars, 1972

This is Bowie's breakout album. It introduced glitter rock, androgyny, and guitar-slinging space aliens to AOR radio. Bowie's wild image aside, songs like "Lady Stardust," "Soul Love," and "Five Years" exhibit a high level of songwriting talent that made Bowie a fixture on the pop charts for decades.

The Carpenters

Close to You, 1970

The Doors

The Very Best of The Doors, 2001

This album shows the sound and fury of Jim Morrison and The Doors featuring the group's number one hits from their short time together.

Bob Dylan

Highway 61 Revisited, 1965

This album takes the listener through Dylan's early electric period, filled with humor ("Highway 61 Revisited"), anger ("Ballad of a Thin Man"), and poetry ("Desolation Row").

The Best of Bob Dylan, 2005

The Eagles

Hotel California, 1976

Their Greatest Hits (1971–1975), 1976

This album features the cool California country rock sounds that inspired generations of musicians and songwriters.

Duke Ellington

The Duke: The Columbia Years (1927–1962), 2000

Fleetwood Mac

Rumours, 1977

Bill Haley & His Comets

The Best of Bill Haley & His Comets, 1999

Jimi Hendrix

Are You Experienced?, 1967

Axis: Bold as Love, 1967

Electric Ladyland, 1968

Hendrix produced only three studio albums—an amazing eight sides of vinyl in only two years—before his tragic death. *Electric Ladyland* is Hendrix at his best with extended jams, psychedelic fuzz tones, wah-wah guitar, and the classic heavy metal version of Bob Dylan's "All Along the Watchtower."

Buddy Holly & The Crickets

The "Chirping" Crickets, 2004

Howlin' Wolf

His Best (Chess 50th Anniversary Collection), 1997

Michael Jackson

Off the Wall, 1979

Thriller, 1982

The best-selling record of all time, this LP captures the pop sound of the early eighties and demonstrates why Michael Jackson was one of the biggest superstars of the twentieth century.

Jefferson Airplane

Surrealistic Pillow, 1967

On the first number-one psychedelic album, Grace Slick's voice swoops and soars through sixties classics like "White Rabbit" and "Somebody to Love," while the Airplane produce trippy folk music that perfectly captured the mood of the era.

Carole King

Tapestry, 1971

With hits including "I Feel the Earth Move," "It's Too Late," and "(You Make Me Feel Like) A Natural Woman," King almost single-handedly invented adult

contemporary rock on this third best-selling album in history.

Lady Gaga

The Fame, 2008

Fame Monster, 2009

Avril Lavigne

Let Go, 2002

On the biggest pop debut of 2002, Lavigne presents an antidote to Britney Spears and other pop divas, wielding her guitar, skateboard, and punk-girl attitude while inspiring a new generation of rockers.

Goodbye Lullaby, 2011

Led Zeppelin

Led Zeppelin IV, 1971

One of the best-selling albums in history thanks to "Stairway to Heaven," this fixture of 1970s AOR radio is classic Zep, combining straight-ahead rock, middle earth mysticism, and heavy metal thunder.

Little Richard

Here's Little Richard, 1957

Madonna

Like a Virgin, 1984

This is the album that made Madonna an international celebrity, and is filled with fun songs, clever wordplay, and irresistible beats.

Barry Manilow

Greatest Hits, 1978

Nirvana

Nevermind, 1991

The hit "Smells Like Teen Spirit" made unlikely pop stars out of Nirvana. The rest of the album is closer to the band's punk origins and perfectly encapsulates the anger and fuzzy sludge of the Seattle grunge sound.

Pink Floyd

Dark Side of the Moon, 1973

Elvis Presley

30 #1 Hits, 2002

This album features Elvis Presley's number-one hits from the pop charts in the United States and in the United Kingdom.

The Complete Million Dollar Quartet, 2006

In December 1956 the biggest stars recording for Sun Records and Elvis Presley, the biggest pop star in the world, got together for an impromptu jam session while the tapes were rolling. Previously released in bits and pieces, this 50th anniversary issue contains twenty minutes of previously unheard music.

Prince

Purple Rain, 1984

The sound track for the Grammy Award-winning movie of the same name, this album is classic Prince with G-rated number-one hits like "When Doves Cry" and "Purple Rain."

Jimmie Rodgers

The Very Best Of, 2009

This album offers the greatest hits by the Singing Brakeman, who put hillbilly music at the top of the pop charts before his untimely death in 1933.

The Rolling Stones

Hot Rocks 1964–1971, 1971

Showcases the Rolling Stones in their prime, with a collection of number one songs that helped cement the group's reputation as the greatest rock band in history.

Frank Sinatra

Classic Sinatra: His Great Performances, 1953–1960, 2000

Bessie Smith

The Very Best Of, 2010

Britney Spears

. . . Baby One More Time, 1999

Femme Fatale, 2011

This is the seventh studio album for Spears, made in collaboration with teen pop songwriter and producer Max Martin. It is filled with unending dance beats that received positive reviews and proved Britney can still please her fans.

Bruce Springsteen

Born in the U.S.A., 1984

Springsteen's dark commentary about the difficult state of life for working Americans in the 1980s is disguised under radio-friendly pop melodies, synthesizers, and happy syncopation.

Tina Turner

Private Dancer, 1984

Various Artists

Saturday Night Fever, 1977

Woodstock, 1994

This live album from the 1969 concert and 1970 film sound track captures the spirit of the times and the music that made history, including Jimi Hendrix's performance of the "Star Spangled Banner" and the debuts of Crosby, Stills & Nash, Santana, and Joe Cocker on the national stage.

Motown 1's, 2004

The Greatest Blues Licks Ever Made, 2008

50s Country, 2010

Hank Williams

20th Century Masters—The Millennium Collection: The Best of Hank Williams, Vol 2, 2006

album: A 12-inch (30cm) vinyl, long-playing (LP) record that holds about twenty minutes of music on each side. In the digital age, an album is also any collection of songs released together by an artist.

beat box: A vocal technique in which a person emulates drumbeats, rhythm, records scratching on turntables, and other musical effects using the mouth, lips, tongue, and voice.

boogie-woogie: A fast-tempo, swinging, or shuffling rhythm used in jazz, rock, and other pop music styles.

chord: A set of notes played simultaneously, as on a guitar or piano.

demographic: Part of a population, such as an age group, gender, or race.

falsetto: A singing method in which the singer uses a voice that is as high as possible.

gold: A term used for records that sell more than five hundred thousand copies.

hook: A memorable melody that catches, or hooks, the listener's attention.

measure: In musical notation, a measure, or bar, is a segment of time defined by a given number of beats.

platinum: A term used to describe re-cords that sell more than 1 million copies. Multiplatinum records sell more than 2 million copies.

producer: In music, a producer works with a band to manage and oversee the recording process.

psychedelic: A word used to describe the hallucinatory effects of the drug LSD, from Greek words that mean to manifest the soul or mind-manifesting.

reggae: A style of Jamaican dance music that originated in the late 1960s and was popularized by Bob Marley in the early 1970s. Reggae is characterized by its strong accent on the offbeat and complex bass lines.

royalty: A percentage of income paid to a creator from the sale of a book, song, or other artistic work.

sampling: The act of taking short portions, or samples, of previously recorded songs and using them for a new song by combining them with other samples or repeating them in a loop.

scat singing: Singing a series of nonsensical words or sounds most often meant to imitate the snarling sounds of a trumpet.

single: A 7-inch (17.7cm) vinyl record with a single song on each side. In the digital age, a single is also any one song that is promoted separately from an album.

syncopation: In pop music, syncopation is a rhythmic style in which the drummer highlights the second and fourth beats, or backbeats, in each four-beat measure.

synthesizer: An electronic instrument, usually played with a keyboard, that produces unique, complex sounds or those that mimic other instruments such as violins and horns.

tenor: A high male singing voice or a man whose voice is in this range.

twelve-bar: One of the most popular chord progressions in popular music, with roots in the blues, wherein each verse occupies twelve bars, or measures, in musical notation.

Books

Justin Bieber. *Justin Bieber: First Step 2 Forever: My Story*. New York: HarperCollins Children's Books, 2010. In this book Bieber tells his own amazing journey from Canadian schoolboy to global superstar.

Hal Marcovitz. *Madonna: Entertainer*. New York: Chelsea House, 2010. This is a complete overview of Madonna's life, insights into her motivations, and her achievements in the context of pop music history.

John Micklos. *Elvis Presley: "I Want to Entertain People."* Berkeley Heights, NJ: Enslow Publishers, 2010. This book recounts the life of a man who entertained for more than two decades, from his debut on *The Ed Sullivan Show* in 1956 to his death in 1977.

Heather Miller. *The Rolling Stones: The Greatest Rock Band*. Berkeley Heights, NJ: Enslow Publishers, 2010. This book profiles each member of the Rolling Stones and describes their passion for American blues music, their role during the rebellious 1960s, and their music, lyrics, and stage antics.

Jeremy Roberts. *The Beatles: Music Revolutionaries*. Minneapolis: Lerner, 2011. This book tells the story of one of the most commercially successful and critically acclaimed acts in the history of popular music. It covers the Beatles journey from Liverpool, England, to the world stage while working in genres ranging from folk rock to psychedelic pop.

Chris Smith. *101 Albums That Changed Popular Music*. New York: Oxford University Press, 2009. This book covers a wide range of blues, jazz, rock, country, hip hop, punk, and alternative albums that influenced pop music from the early 1950s to the 1990s.

Websites

AllMusic (www.allmusic.com). Originally known as the All Music Guide (AMG), the AllMusic website is one of the most comprehensive music guides on the Internet. The site has in-depth information about old music, classics, and the latest hits, as well as descriptions of genres from opera to punk.

Billboard.com (www.billboard.com). This is *Billboard* magazine's website. It features music, news, reviews, and the latest Hot 100, Billboard 200,

R&B/Hip Hop, Digital Songs, and Pop Songs charts.

MTV (www.mtv.com). This website for the original music video TV channel features artist biographies, interviews, online games, and dozens of music videos that can be streamed online.

Pop Culture Madness: Pop Music News (www.popculturemadness.com /Music). This flashy website features the latest pop music news, free song downloads, information about the top pop songs from the *Billboard* charts dating back to the 1950s, and hundreds of pages about fashion, films, TV, and celebrities.

Rolling Stone (www.rollingstone.com). *Rolling Stone* has been covering pop stars and the music industry since the 1960s. The magazine's website contains the latest music and pop culture news, biographies of everyone from Hank Williams to Justin Bieber, and music, movie, and video reviews and downloads.

INDEX

Hammer, M.C., 101
Harris, Peppermint, 31
Harrison, George, 50–55, *51*, *54*
Heavy metal music, 71, 73, 96–97
Henderson, Fletcher, 25
Hendrix, Jimi, 45–46, 60, 63–64, 71, 92
Henley, Don, 76–77, *76*
Hip hop, 100–102, 104–105
Hippies, 52–53, 58, 68
Holland, Brian, 49–50
Holland, Eddie, 49–50
Holly, Buddy, 43, 50
Honky-tonk music, 28–29, 33, 67
Howlin' Wolf, 35
Hughes, Langston, 18

I

Ice-T, 103–104
Internet, 6, 98
iTunes, 6, 62

J

Jackson, Bullmoose, 31
Jackson, Michael, 26, 85–86, *85*, 96, 112
James, Rick, 84, 101
Jardine, Al, 46
Jazz, 6, 19–26
Jefferson Airplane, 58, 60, 63
Jennings, Waylon, 67
Jimi Hendrix Experience, 60, 92
Johnson, Lonnie, 18
Jolicoeur, David Jude, *101*
Jonas Brothers, 115
Jones, John Paul, 71
Joplin, Janis, *59*, 60–61, 63
Joplin, Scott, 14

K

Keisker, Marion, 35
King, B.B., 35

King, Carole, *47*, 48, 67–68
Koppel, Ted, 82

L

La Rocca, Nick, 20
Lady Gaga, 8, *114*, 115–116
Lavigne, Avril, 110–112, *111*
Leadon, Bernie, 76, 77
Led Zeppelin, 71–73, *72*
Lennon, John, 46–47, 50–55, *51*, *54*, 63–64
Lewis, Jerry Lee, 37, 38, 43
Lil' Kim, 105
Little Eva, 48
Little Richard (Richard Penniman), 26, 39, *40*, 41, 45, 46, 50, 55, 102
LL Cool J, 102
Love, Mike, 46
LP albums, 55
Lynyrd Skynyrd, 67

M

Madonna, 8, 26, 78, 86–88, *88*, 90, 94, 97, 110, 116
Manilow, Barry, 66–67, 78
Mann, Barry, 48
Marley, Bob, 92
Marshall Tucker Band, 67
Martin, George, 52, 53
Mason, Vincent, *101*
Maudsley, Frank, *83*
McCartney, Paul, 50–55, *51*, *54*, 85
McVie, Christine, 75
McVie, John, 75
Meisner, Randy, 76, 77
Mercer, Kevin, *101*
Miller, Glenn, 25
Mintz, Leo, 31
Moore, Scotty, 35
Morrison, Jim, 61, 63
Motown, 48–50, 62, 64, 107

S

T

V

W

Y

PICTURE CREDITS

Stuart A. Kallen is the author of more than 250 nonfiction books for children and young adults. He has written extensively about science, the environment, music, history, and folklore (from vampires to haunted houses). In addition, Mr. Kallen has written award-winning children's videos and television scripts. In his spare time, he sings, writes songs, and plays the guitar. Kallen lives in San Diego, California.